The Key Elements for Classroom Management

The Key Elements of Classroom Management

Managing Time and Space, Student Behavior, and Instructional Strategies

Joyce McLeod   Jan Fisher   Ginny Hoover

Association for Supervision and Curriculum Development
Alexandria, Virginia USA

Association for Supervision and Curriculum Development
1703 N. Beauregard St. • Alexandria, VA 22311-1714 USA
Telephone: 800-933-2723 or 703-578-9600 • Fax: 703-575-5400
Web site: http://www.ascd.org • E-mail: member@ascd.org

Gene R. Carter, *Executive Director;* Nancy Modrak, *Director of Publishing;* Julie Houtz, *Director of Book Editing & Production;* Ernesto Yermoli, *Project Manager;* Shelley Young, *Senior Graphic Designer;* Valerie Sprague and Keith Demmons, *Desktop Publishing Specialists;* Tracey A. Smith, *Production Manager.*

Printed in the United States of America.

ISBN: 0-87120-787-7   ASCD product no.: 103008
ASCD member price: $20.95   nonmember price: $25.95   s9/03

Library of Congress Cataloging-in-Publication Data

McLeod, Joyce, 1940–
   The key elements of classroom management : Managing time and space, student
behavior, and instructional strategies / Joyce McLeod, Jan Fisher, and
Ginny Hoover.
       p. cm.
Includes bibliographical references and index.
   ISBN 0-87120-787-7 (alk. paper)
   1. Classroom management. I. Fisher, Jan, 1930- II. Hoover, Ginny,
1946- III. Title.

   LB3013.M386 2003
   371.102'4—dc21

                              2003012528

13 12 11 10 09 08 07 06 05 04 03   12 11 10 9 8 7 6 5 4 3 2 1

Preface

How can we judge the worth of society? If the children and youth of a nation are afforded the opportunity to develop their capacities to the fullest, if they are given the knowledge to understand the world and the wisdom to change it, then the prospects for the future are bright.

—Urie Bronfenbrenner (1970)

Bronfenbrenner's quote underscores the critical role teachers play in affecting the future of our nation. It is the teacher's responsibility to provide the instructional program and classroom environment that allow each child to develop his or her capacities to the fullest. Yet, in today's classrooms, teachers are frustrated that the strategies that may have worked for them in the past are not working now. Statements like these seem to echo throughout the teaching profession:

- "If only I had more time!"
- "I can't fit another table, desk, or chair in this classroom!"
- "Teach? You've got to be kidding! I spend all my time trying to control the kids!"
- "My students just didn't get what I taught yesterday. What am I going to do today?"

If you have made these statements once or twice, know that you are not alone! Too many times classroom management issues overwhelm both new and experienced teachers. Yet, a well-organized and efficiently managed classroom is the essential foundation upon which to build a solid instructional program and a climate of mutual respect and caring between students and teachers. In fact, an analysis of research done over the last 50 years clearly shows that the teacher's classroom management abilities have more of an effect on student learning than any other category analyzed (Wang, Haertel, & Walberg, 1993–1994).

The basic role of the teacher is to be the instructional leader. In order to fulfill that role, the teacher must deal with the social, intellectual, and physical structure of the classroom. Classroom life involves planning the curriculum; organizing routine procedures; gathering resources; arranging the environment to maximize efficiency; monitoring student progress; and anticipating, preventing, and solving problems.

Perhaps it is time to take a fresh look at classroom management. In analyzing the work of the teacher, these three key elements stand out as critical components of a well-managed classroom:

- Efficient use of time and classroom space
- Implementation of strategies that influence students to make good choices, rather than ones that attempt to control student behavior
- Wise choice and effective implementation of instructional strategies

In discussing the book's organization and content, the authors became convinced that a book organized around these three key elements allows us to share strategies and pose solutions to some of the most perplexing classroom management problems. For example, student misbehavior may, in many instances, result from the lack of space in which to work rather than from a deeply rooted behavior problem. So by focusing on setting up the classroom to anticipate students' space needs, problem behaviors may be prevented.

Taking a proactive approach to building relationships between the teacher and students, among students, and between the teacher and parents ensures that students participate in a learning community based on mutual respect and caring. Students who have a role in building a positive classroom environment are much more likely to assume responsibility for their own behavior and become good role models for others.

Evaluating instructional strategies and matching them to the students' academic needs and learning styles increase the likelihood of higher student achievement. Students whose learning needs are being met are likely to feel competent and a part of the classroom community and, therefore, much less likely to exhibit behavior problems. So the theme of this book is that good classroom management strategies increase student achievement and prevent both learning problems and behavior problems (which are usually related). Our goal is to present strategies that make the teacher's work easier and allow more time to focus on the instructional program rather than on routine management issues and individual behavior problems.

The contents of the book are ordered to align with the flow of the teacher's work. In Section 1, we present strategies and ideas for setting up the classroom, deciding how instructional time will be scheduled, determining routine classroom procedures, organizing materials for easy access, and making good use of teacher time. In Section 2, we present strategies for developing relationships with each student so that the atmosphere of "teacher in control" is changed to one in which students make choices and accept responsibility for those choices. In Section 3, we discuss research-based instructional strategies, identifying their advantages and disadvantages and relating them to use in whole-class, small group, partner, or individual settings.

Because each chapter is designed to address a critical issue within the key elements of classroom management, readers can elect to read the book as a whole or use it as a desk reference or as a guide for professional development. It is our hope that our book helps you in your day-to-day quest to provide an effectively managed classroom.

Time and Classroom Space

Joyce McLeod

Managing Time and Classroom Space

The efficient use of time is an important variable in helping students achieve learning goals and making the classroom a pleasant place for teachers and students. Unfortunately, how you spend your time is all too often determined by state or district mandates, school policy, and rigid daily school schedules. Instructional strategies must be planned to fit into fixed time frames, where it is the clock—and not your assessment of whether students need more time on a topic—that dictates the beginning and end of a lesson.

The present emphasis on standards and high-stakes assessment also affects how time is allocated in the school day. Most standards-based curricula are rigorous courses of study that, in most instances, specify achievement of many more objectives than can be taught to an appropriate depth. This results in teachers spending their days reviewing material that students have not yet fully mastered while simultaneously being pressured to move on to other objectives. Many students are not even ready for the mandated grade-level curriculum when they enter the classroom, so instructional time has to be stretched like a rubber band to teach all students so that they can be successful on the high-stakes test. Other variables that affect your use of time include noninstructional routine procedures, transitions between activities or classes, and schoolwide interruptions. But time is not the only issue; classroom space affects your instructional program directly as well. Teachers try to make every inch of classroom space count in order to have a rich and inviting classroom environment because they know that the richness of students' experiences are enhanced or diminished by their surroundings. The organization of space also affects the way students behave and move around the classroom, as well as how much attention they pay to instruction.

A high-quality instructional program, then, requires efficient use of time and space. It necessitates a classroom rich in accessible, well-organized materials and inviting spaces where students can work alone, in groups, and with you.

The purpose of Chapter 1–4 is to present strategies and techniques to help you ensure that your students spend most of their class time engaged in learning and that your classroom space is used as efficiently as possible. You rarely have the opportunity to make more time for learning or to stretch the walls for more classroom space. But teachers have always demonstrated that they are remarkably creative at making good use of whatever resources they have, and it is the goal of this section to help you do that.

—*Joyce McLeod*

1

Setting Up the Classroom

We never educate directly, but indirectly by means of the environment.

—John Dewey (1944)

This is a new year and a new beginning. Whether you are returning to a school in which you are a veteran teacher, beginning your career as a new teacher, or a veteran teacher teaching in a new building, setting up your classroom space is the first assignment of a new school year. The way you set up your classroom largely determines the experiences you and your students share.

Deciding what type of seating arrangement you want depends upon the type of furniture you have, the space in your classroom, and your style of teaching. Other important decisions include determining the types of spaces you need for group and ongoing activities, individual workspaces, and permanent storage of materials and records. Your classroom's visual appearance depends on what you do with bulletin boards, chalkboards, other wall spaces, and even the door to your classroom. Visitors form their first impressions of you and your classroom climate by observing the displays and the classroom arrangement.

Another important consideration is establishing traffic patterns to make movement in, out, and around your classroom efficient. Safety regulations and fire codes require that exits not be blocked and traffic patterns be established for emergency exit. In this chapter we examine the factors that facilitate the creation of a pleasing and efficient learning environment.

Taking Inventory

What furniture and equipment do you *have* and what do you *need?* Hopefully, you have your class list so you know how many students are starting the year with you and what subjects you are teaching. Make a written inventory of the furniture and equipment you have. Use a form, such as the one in Figure 1.1, to record your inventory.

Figure 1.1
Furniture and Equipment Inventory

Type of Furniture or Equipment	Number on Hand	Number Needed
Desks		
Chairs		

Arranging Student Seating

Because you usually don't know your students at the beginning of the year, it is difficult to assign seats before the first few weeks of school; however, it is important to place the furniture in configurations that work with your teaching style and available space. If you know that your class includes students with disabilities, such as those with poor vision, hearing impairment, or who need wheelchairs or other assistive devices, consider the accommodations you need to make in your classroom arrangement when you begin your planning. Here are some key ideas to keep in mind:

- Accommodate the type of instruction and activities you use most often
- Be flexible so that students can easily and quickly rearrange furniture to accommodate a special activity
- Allow space for student movement, storage, and equipment setups
- Encourage movement and flexibility
- Provide a maximum amount of personal space for each student

Teachers are well aware of the problems caused when too many students are housed in too small a space. Research done many years ago on classroom density clearly shows that crowded classrooms affect students' attitudes and conduct by increasing dissatisfaction and aggression and decreasing attentiveness (Weinstein, 1979). However, the research emphasis in recent years has shifted to the effect of class size on student achievement, rather than the effect of classroom density on both achievement and behavior. This research has yielded mixed results, with no definitive answer as to the effect of smaller class sizes on student achievement and behavior. Perhaps more research attention should be given to the issue of classroom density to determine the effect of the space available on each student's achievement and behavior.

Requisitioning new furniture or equipment is much easier if you have an inventory of what you presently have to use as a rationale for your needs.

In the traditional arrangement of students in rows of desks and chairs, students in the front and center are more likely to participate and be called on by the teacher. Therefore, well-planned seating arrangements and placement of students who need help maintaining their focus in the front and center of the seating arrangement encourage these students to pay attention and participate (Edwards, 1993).

In planning your classroom arrangement, consider grouping students into sections with walkways from the back to the front and side-to-side between the rows. This allows you to move easily around in the classroom, check students' progress, and send the subtle message that students should stay on task. This type of arrangement can be quickly rearranged so that students can work together in small groups. Figures 1.2, 1.3, and 1.4 show possible arrangements for primary (preK–2), elementary (grades 3–6), middle, and high school classrooms.

Figure 1.2
Primary Grades Classroom Arrangement

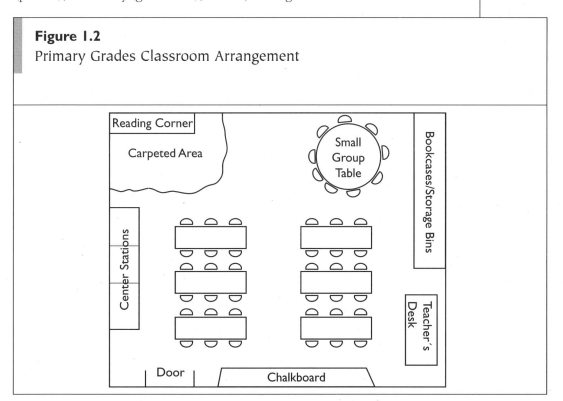

Figure 1.3
Upper Elementary Grades Classroom Arrangement

Figure 1.4
Middle and High School Classroom Arrangement

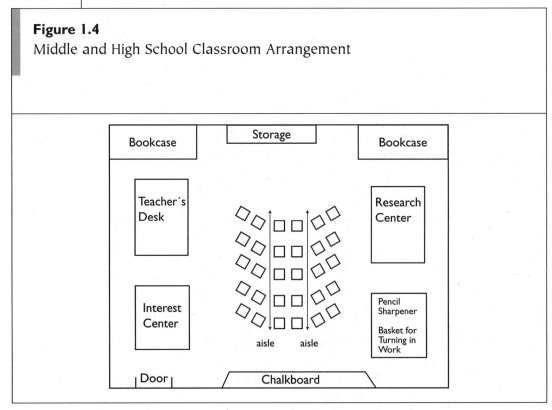

Another major consideration in arranging student seating is the area of each student's personal space. The dimensions of the room, the number of students, and the necessary work and storage areas determine this.

Consider the time students spend sitting in their assigned seats versus the time they spend in various other areas of the classroom to determine whether you should scale back the space for some special areas to provide each student more personal space.

Placing Your Desk

Now that you have arranged student seating, think about placement of your desk. The following considerations may help you:

- Placing your desk in the *back* of the classroom promotes a student-centered environment and provides workspace for you while allowing you to keep an eye on your students. Students can talk with you without being observed by others.
- Placing your desk in the *front* of the classroom promotes a teacher-directed environment and allows you to see most areas of the classroom and monitor students at work. It does not, however, allow for private conferences with individual students.
- Placing your desk in the *center* of the student seating arrangement promotes a teacher-facilitated environment. Students have easy access to your desk, but private conversations are not possible.
- Placing your desk off to the *side* of the classroom sends a message that your desk is your personal workspace. Private conversations are possible in this arrangement.

The placement of your desk also depends on the subjects you teach, the age of the students, and the available space. In middle and high school classrooms, teachers may place their desks off to the side in the front of the room. The desk may be grouped with file cabinets and storage cabinets to provide easy access to materials from the teaching area in the front of the room and the ability to monitor students working independently.

In elementary classrooms, teachers decide about placement of their desks based on their personal philosophy of instruction and the classroom seating arrangement. Most primary teachers place their desks in an out-of-the-way place so that they have maximum space for students to sit on the floor in a large circle. After you have arranged student seating and placed your desk, sit in each desk to make sure that each student has a good line of sight to the chalkboard, the front of the room,

To find the area of each student's personal space, measure the dimensions of your room and then find the area. As you arrange the various working areas of your room, estimate the area needed for each and subtract it from the total area. Divide the remaining area by the number of students to find the area of each student's space.

or other critical areas.

Even more important than the placement of your desk is how your desk looks—not just on that first day of school but every single day. A neatly arranged desk with interesting objects, such as a plant, a pencil holder, or a family picture, sends a clear message to students that you value neatness and order and that you are willing to share some personal aspects of your life. A disorderly desk piled high with books, papers, and other "stuff" sends a clear message that you are not well organized and may not hold students accountable for neatness in their work.

Now let's turn our attention to arranging other key areas in your classroom.

Instructional Areas

Special areas make your classroom interesting and communicate your instructional goals to students, administrators, and visitors. In most elementary schools and in some middle and high schools, the following areas may be a part of the classroom: learning centers and interest centers, small-group meeting areas, individual work-spaces, computer stations, materials storage, and records storage.

Learning Centers and Interest Centers

An interest center is designed to encourage student activity and choice during free time; a learning center is designed to meet specific learning objectives. Interest centers invite student choice; learning centers motivate, reinforce, and support student learning (Lemlech, 1991).

In this era of high-stakes testing, learning centers are valuable tools to review, reinforce, and provide ongoing practice on critical standards. Interest centers allow students free choice and motivate students to pursue personal interests. For example, an interest center focused on encouraging students to read for pleasure and for information of personal interest might contain trade books chosen by the students. The student choosing the book puts a bookmark in it explaining why she chose it, and subsequent readers add bookmarks describing their reactions to the book. The table in Figure 1.5 defines the steps for setting up and maintaining a learning center.

Most elementary classrooms have interest centers, such as a reading corner, a game area, or a science center. Middle and high school classrooms might set up such centers for current events or reading materials related to the subject area. Interest centers enrich the classroom curriculum. As shown in Figure 1.6, setting up an interest center requires different decision-making steps than those used to set up a learning center.

Figure 1.5
Setting Up a Learning Center

Step 1	Define the instructional objective for the center.
Step 2	Decide what activity is appropriate, how students will interact, and what they will do. Estimate the amount of time a student should be at the center.
Step 3	Gather the necessary resources and materials. Post clear directions in the center so that students can work independently. Develop a system so that students know what they are to do and for how long they may work at the center.
Step 4	Decide how to evaluate students' work and how students will know that they have completed the work required. Include that information in the directions.
Step 5	Decide how many days or weeks the center will be used and whether it must be completely replaced, moved, rearranged, or simply the activity changed to further develop the instructional objective.

Figure 1.6
Setting Up an Interest Center

Step 1	Define the goals of the center. Is the main purpose to motivate students, to enhance instruction in a subject area(s), to develop thinking skills, or some other goal?
Step 2	Decide what students are to do. Will students work together or individually? About how long will students need to work in the center?
Step 3	Gather the necessary resources and materials. Post clear directions so that students can work independently. Develop a system so they know when they may work at the center and for how long.
Step 4	Decide what, if any, record students should keep of their work. Provide a format for students to record appropriate information, such as the date of their visit, amount of time spent, a brief description of their work, and an evaluation of what they learned.
Step 5	Decide whether the center can be ongoing throughout the year, such as a Reading Corner, and how often materials and directions should be changed.

Small-Group Meeting Area

Locate the small-group meeting area away from individual work areas so as not to disturb students working independently. Furnish the area with chairs and a large worktable and locate it close to a bulletin board and storage and supply area. Post rules or guidelines for small-group work in the work area.

Effective group work is the result of careful teaching of appropriate skills for working together and a classroom arrangement conducive to group work. For a more complete discussion of the many different types of group work, see Section 3 of this book.

In middle and high school classrooms, students work independently in small group settings to complete projects and presentations. The key to successful group work is to provide

- Focused instruction on how to work with a small group.
- Clear directions for the task or project.
- Accessible materials.
- A timeline for completing the work.
- Information on how the group's work is evaluated.

In elementary school classrooms, teachers meet with small groups for direct instruction, particularly in reading. Teachers may use a combination of small-group meetings for guided reading and discussion with independent work or center work going on simultaneously, so the group area should be located away from learning and interest centers and the seating area. However, teachers should have a direct line of sight to all areas of the room from the small-group meeting space.

Primary and elementary teachers move slowly toward independent small-group work based on students' developmental characteristics. Primary teachers generally begin group work by having partners work together in a very short "think-pair-share" activity. Students remain in the seating area, and the teacher directs the activity from the front of the room. In later years, small-group work moves toward having students assume more responsibility for working with classmates without direct teacher intervention. This necessitates teaching students what skills are appropriate for working in groups as well as how to rearrange the classroom by turning desks together or grouping tables and chairs.

Individual Workspaces

Individual workspaces are critically important for students in all grades. Having sufficient personal space helps students avoid the stress of other students "invading" their space and engaging in unnecessary conversation and disagreements. Students who have difficulty concentrating in a crowded area or who exhibit persistent behavior problems need a larger space or a space removed from those of most other students. These workspaces can be single desks moved away from the main seating area or study carrels, which allow students to have a defined space with sight barriers on three sides. Study carrels are particularly useful for students who exhibit symptoms of attention deficit disorder and hyperactivity.

In some classrooms, areas are partitioned off with moveable bulletin boards, bookcases, or other pieces of furniture. Individual desks are usually placed in these areas, and only a few students work there at any one time. In many cases, these areas are used as "time out" or "cooling off" areas for students who are having difficulties. These areas should be used as temporary seating, and all students should understand that their purpose is to help students solve their problems and regain control, not just to punish them for misdeeds. We have found that offering students the choice to move to such an area if they feel they need time apart from the group prevents problems.

Computer Stations

As technology assumes a larger role in the classroom instructional program, space, proper lighting, wiring, and Internet hookups are becoming necessities. Arrangement is determined by whether the computers are placed on desks or worktables, in a defined area or at each student's personal workspace. In most elementary classrooms, there are usually a few computers placed in one area of the classroom and perhaps a computer lab for the entire school. In middle and high schools, there may be both computer labs and classrooms in which every student is seated at a computer station. Regardless of the configuration, the following guidelines should be considered:

- If computers play a pervasive role in the instructional program, design the layout of classroom workstations ergonomically, with adequate space for hardware, proper lighting, wiring placed out of traffic areas, and chairs that promote good posture.
- Implement a security program that minimizes theft and vandalism.
- Post basic instructions and rules governing computer use at each station or at a central location visible from all stations. If you plan to interact with students while they are seated at computers, make sure that you can maintain eye contact with students. Ask students to stand briefly while instructions are being given.
- Arrange computers so that students cannot easily see other monitors if the computer is used for online testing or individualized instruction. Provide more space between computers if students share terminals. Make accommodations in the arrangement if you have students who need wheelchair access or who are visually impaired.
- Allow sufficient space so that you can easily move around the computers, and the area can be safely and quickly evacuated in case of an emergency.
- Place desks in rows, an L-shaped or U-shaped arrangement, or clusters of four to six desks for greater efficiency.

Computer Classroom Design: The Issues Facing Designers of Computer Classrooms, an online article available at http://www.workspace-resources.com/ education/cicdesi1.htm, provides helpful resources for setting up computer labs and individual workstations. In his article "Planning the Multimedia Classroom," Larry Buchanan (1996) defines the goals and objectives of a multiyear technology plan for the McMinn County Schools in Tennessee and provides guidelines for classroom layout and choosing technology components and other furniture.

Effective use of hands-on materials, such as math manipulatives and science equipment, is directly related to how efficiently they are stored and managed. For example, you are much more likely to use manipulatives in your math lessons if they are stored in a convenient location, packaged in quantities sufficient for the activity, and checked for missing or broken pieces. Well-organized manipulatives and equipment make for successful lessons.

Materials Storage

Other important areas are those in which you store materials: bookcases, closed cabinets, bins, and any other creative storage systems you may have. Placing storage systems near the area where they are frequently used minimizes lost time. Teaching students which storage areas are off limits is also critical to effective classroom management.

Students in all grades can be taught an efficient system to pass out and collect materials, count to be sure all materials have been returned, and replace the materials neatly in their proper containers. Research clearly shows that students learn best when they "do" rather than just "listen and read," so effective management of materials is fundamental to a good instructional program and key to good classroom management.

Records Storage

A locked cabinet is a necessity for the secure storage of student records: report cards, permanent record folders, standardized test results, anecdotal records, grade books, portfolios, and so forth. It is sensible to keep the key to that cabinet in a secure place and never allow student access to it. Avoid storing anything in that file cabinet that a substitute teacher, parent volunteer, or instructional aide might need. Because some records may be stored on the computer, the teacher's responsibility also includes ensuring that these records are secure and stored according to school and district policy. ·

Now that you have completed arranging the basic areas of your classroom, consider how to make the room visually attractive.

Visual Displays

Learning is a sensory experience. The main channels through which we take in information are through our eyes (visual), ears (auditory), and fingers (kinesthetic). We learn best through concrete experiences—the kinesthetic modality. The visual displays in your classroom are also powerful learning tools, so you should plan them very carefully.

Ask yourself whether your display

- Provides information about school and classroom routines.
- Supports concepts and skills that you are *presently* teaching. (Nothing is less interesting to students than a bulletin board that is months old and that has no relevance to current instruction.)
- Presents information in a way different from other learning materials. (For example, a graphic of the structure of a short story is helpful if it

is referred to in daily instruction and not readily available in print materials.)

- Graphically illustrates fundamental concepts. (For example, place-value models showing the relationships of place-value positions illustrate a math concept fundamental to work with whole numbers.)

Bulletin Boards

Informational bulletin boards designed for the first few weeks of school help students in the upper elementary grades through high school get basic information about school life, including:

- Map of the school, classroom rules, the daily schedule, lunch prices, and menus
- Bus schedules and morning and afternoon pickup locations, location of carpool and after-school care transportation pickup, parking rules (for high school students), and location of bicycle racks
- Location and date of assignment of lockers
- The style of paper heading you require

If you have a class meeting for the purpose of developing classroom rules, announce that meeting by placing a sign where the rules will be posted. When students are asked at the beginning of the year what concerns they have, their answers almost always relate to basic routines, schedules, and locations of important places—restrooms, lunchroom, lockers, other classrooms, and so forth. Providing this information in a visual format helps students get information without having to ask you.

Instructional bulletin boards have great potential to enhance learning. The human eyes contain almost 70 percent of the body's sensory receptors and send millions of signals every second along the optic nerves to the visual processing centers of the brain. Not only do we take in more information visually than through any of the other senses, we also have a much greater capacity for long-term memory of pictures (Wolfe, 2001). Visuals also guide understanding. Think of trying to understand the water cycle, the structure of an atom, or even the layout of the school without the aid of a visual.

Map out the major curricular units you teach during the year. Think about the types of visual displays most effective for each unit. Consider the amount of teacher and student time required to make each display, the materials needed, and the instructional value of each display. Planning ahead helps you make better use of materials and your time in preparing displays.

Protecting the Privacy of Student Records: Guidelines for Education Agencies (National Center for Education Statistics, 1997) is an excellent source of information on the legal requirements for maintaining confidential student information. Other helpful resources include *First Class GradeBook (2003)*—computer software with the capability to transfer data between the school office, district, and home. A review of this software is available online at http://www.winplanet.com/winplanet/reviews/654/1/screenshot314.

Graphic organizers are visual tools that enhance learning. Well-planned bulletin boards and other visual displays support your classroom curriculum and provide information about school life.

In her book *Visual Literacy: Learn to See, See to Learn,* Lynell Burmark (2002) provides comprehensive guidelines on use of type and color and ideas for various types of classroom displays.

Use the following guidelines to develop a rich visual environment in your classroom:

- Focus each display on one easily illustrated objective that represents critical content. Research on how the brain learns clearly shows that students remember visuals longer than information presented verbally. Even after the visual is removed, students' recall is better when they are in the room where the display was located (Sprenger, 1999).
- Use a short title that conveys the major intent of the display. Use initial capitals and lowercase letters for titles because students read these much more easily than words in all capitals. Choose a clean letter style that matches the typeface students see in their print materials, rather than using very decorative letter cutouts.
- Choose bulletin board borders that are not busy and brightly colored because they detract from the display itself and are not helpful to students who have difficulty focusing on essential information.
- Choose a background color that provides a sharp contrast between the background and the items placed on it. Assess the lighting in the area of your bulletin board. If it is in a dark area, choose light-colored backgrounds. If there is intense light in the area, dark backgrounds work well.
- Include bulletin boards that students either create or on which they have the option to display their own work.

The time you spend planning and preparing the visual displays in your classroom is time well spent. Student achievement is enhanced when the walls "teach."

Traffic Patterns

Now that you have everything in place in your classroom, think about how students will move around the room and how they will enter and leave it.

Moving Around in the Classroom

Identify the areas to which you allow students free access, such as the supply cabinets or shelves, pencil sharpener, interest centers, and the location for turning in completed work. Notice where each of these areas is in relation to learning centers and small-group and student seating areas. If you have space, locate the free-access areas far enough away from these work areas so that students are not walking directly into or around them. If your classroom is simply too small to allow students free access to different areas, explain this and set specific times for pencil sharpening and getting necessary supplies. Use that time for a stretch break—a good strategy for helping students relax, refresh, and refocus.

Another key traffic pattern is the movement when a small-group activity ends and another begins, such as when a teacher releases one reading group and calls another. Using a circular flow works well: have students leaving the group walk toward the front of the room and then turn to go to their seats, while the arriving group walks toward the back of the room and then turns toward the group meeting area. It never hurts to have students take a short walk to their next activity.

Teach students to walk toward the *back* of the room when *going to* their assigned learning center, interest area, or small-group area and toward the *front* when *leaving* a group activity. If you rotate activities on a time schedule, have students move to their next activity in a clockwise direction.

The key to establishing and maintaining good traffic flow in the classroom is taking the time to teach the pattern and have students practice it. Even in middle and high school classrooms, practice is still a good idea. Throughout the year, take a few minutes now and again to reevaluate the traffic flow in the classroom, make changes if needed, and review with students the new procedures or the ones that you have had in place. Establishing good traffic patterns saves valuable class time, minimizes opportunities for off-task behavior, and allows students more opportunities to move around to meet their personal needs.

Entering and Leaving the Classroom

For middle and high school teachers, this event happens at least hourly and has the potential for helping you begin and end each class with order or chaos, depending on your procedures. Perhaps the most important elements in making class changes orderly are your presence at the classroom door and the procedure you have in place for entering and leaving. The most successful strategy is to have entering students line up against the wall outside of the classroom while the present class leaves. However, this isn't possible in many schools because students need to get to lockers in the hall, and students standing in front of the lockers cause confusion and possible misbehavior. So, the next option is to have departing students move to the back of the classroom and walk up the side of the room to their right and exit, while the entering students come in, turn right, walk down the side of the classroom on their right, and then turn to go to their assigned seats. If there are materials that students need to use and return at the end of class, establish a location and a traffic pattern to allow students to pick them up as they are going to their seats.

Even though secondary students are generally not asked to move through the halls in lines, there are times when orderly lines are important. When the entire student body attends an assembly, a procedure for lining up in an orderly fashion saves time and prevents behavior problems. Make sure that groups of students

One of my most successful bulletin boards was a very simple one titled "Works in Progress." Students were invited to share drafts of their writing and ask for feedback from their peers. The only things I placed on the bulletin board were the class-generated rules for "How to Give Constructive Criticism." Another wonderful advantage is that it remained up all year and changed almost daily.

who tend to misbehave do not line up together and do not change their positions in line. Make it clear to students that they cannot get out of the line to sit with students in other classes, that they must fill every seat in a row, and that they need to follow teachers' directions for entering and leaving the assembly.

The lunchroom is another area in high school and middle school that requires orderly lines. The best option is to use roped-off lines to keep students moving in an orderly fashion and to make breaking in line difficult. If this is not possible, designate a place for the line to form that is out of a high traffic area. As a general rule, students should be taught that if a line forms in a high traffic area, such as at the water fountain or at the door of a crowded restroom, they should stand against the wall out of the traffic flow.

In primary and elementary classrooms, there are many times when the entire class lines up and leaves the classroom or when students return from special classes, such as physical education, art, music, or library. Work with the teachers of these special classes to set up a standard procedure for returning to your classroom. Procedures for lining up minimize the "race to be first." If students sit at tables or desk groups, give each table or group a number or a name that you use to call groups to line up. Criteria for the order of selection can be based on any scheme that works for you, but be sure that each table gets an equal opportunity to be first in line.

When your students return from special classes, particularly physical education, they tend to be excited and talkative and in need of time to settle down. It helps if you allow them time to get water and go to the restroom. Have students form a line outside the classroom to wait their turn to go to the water fountain and restrooms and then to their seats. In that way, some students remain in the line so as not to overcrowd the restroom facilities or create a long line at the water fountain. Pushing and shoving in the water fountain line have caused more than one cut lip and broken tooth.

Another good way to settle students down before reentering the classroom is to have a quick activity as they stand in line. For example, you can use standing-in-line time to help elementary students practice their listening skills. Whisper a fact about something students are studying to the first person in line. Have the fact whispered from student to student down the line. Have the last person share the "fact." Discuss what happened to the fact as it traveled down the line and how communication can sometimes be misunderstood.

If your students have been in a class that requires sitting for the majority of the time, take a few minutes to stretch or sing a song to reenergize them. Elementary students have short attention spans and difficulty sitting for long periods of time, so using a few minutes for settling down and then having them follow an established traffic pattern back into the classroom prepares them for the next activity.

Summary

Some of your most important work is already complete. You have

- Established your classroom environment.
- Thought carefully about how to arrange seating and create spaces for special activities.
- Considered your curriculum and what kinds of visual displays best support your instructional program.
- Established traffic patterns that help students move around in your classroom and enter and leave it so that you minimize disruptions and lost time.
- Thought about how to ensure privacy of student records, and established a place where you can talk privately with individual students.
- Created a classroom that invites your students in, makes them comfortable and, most importantly, provides a physical environment conducive to learning.

In Chapter 2, we will examine strategies for using instructional time effectively, focusing on how use of time relates to choice of instructional strategies. The time spent planning and creating your physical environment yields dividends as you manage that precious resource of engaged learning time.

2 Managing Instructional Time

Until we can manage TIME, we can manage nothing else.
                                    —Peter F. Drucker (1954)

The clock seems to manage every school day. The daily schedule is based on a variety of factors, such as state- or district-mandated time periods for a given subject, bus schedules, local school schedules for special classes, lunch periods, and teacher planning time. Wong and Wong (1998) describe four different types of school-day time:

1. **Allocated time.** The total time for teacher instruction and student learning
2. **Instructional time.** The time teachers are actively teaching
3. **Engaged time.** The time students are involved in a task
4. **Academic learning time.** The time teachers can prove that students learned the content or mastered the skill

In this chapter, we examine some basic daily schedules used in a variety of elementary, middle, and high school settings and look at ways to use this scheduled time to maximize instructional time. Time management is critical to student achievement and attitudes toward learning.

The Daily Schedule: Elementary School

Elementary school schedules are generally determined by three factors: the number of instructional minutes for each subject area as mandated by the district or state; special class schedules, such as music, art, physical education, and library; and the overall school schedule as dictated by bus schedules, lunch times, and so forth.

Time frames for each subject area in the elementary grades vary according to grade level, but the largest block of the daily schedule is usually devoted to reading and language arts and the second largest block to mathematics. The remaining subject areas—science, social studies, health, music, art, and physical education—may have mandates for a certain number of minutes per day or week, but the schedule is usually left to the discretion of the local school if special teachers teach art, music, or physical education, or to each teacher or team of teachers for scheduling science, social studies, and health.

The school day for kindergarten is usually either a half-day or full-day program. Kindergarten schedules are therefore individualized within these time frames and developed according to the philosophy that guides the program. However, for some kindergarten classes (usually the full-day programs), the schedule is also driven by the overall school schedule for lunch, bus schedules, and special classes, such as music, art, and physical education.

Looping

One successful way of organizing the elementary school, and even the middle school, to make better use of instructional time is the practice of looping. In this approach, students remain with one teacher for two to three years—the teacher and the students get promoted together. According to Jim Grant, codirector of the National Alliance of Multiage Educators, teachers who loop have fewer transitions to make at the beginning of the school year and can introduce curriculum topics right a way. By allowing students and teachers to remain together, Grant says, looping buys time (Rasmussen, 1998). This extra time allows teachers to teach topics in greater depth and to better meet the needs of individual students.

Vertical Teams

Another organizational option in the elementary grades is the vertical team. In this configuration, one team of teachers teaches multiple grade levels in a "neighborhood" concept. The same children remain in the neighborhood with this team of teachers for a period of four to five years. Just as in the looping strategy, time spent getting to know students at the beginning of the year, teaching routines and procedures, and assessing each student's learning level are eliminated. Teachers have the benefit of knowing the students they will teach the following year; in addition,

According to research reported in Wong and Wong (1998), the typical teacher consumes 90 percent of allocated time. Yet the only way a student learns anything is by putting in effort—by learning to work.

Red Mountain Ranch
School in Mesa, Arizona,
is incorporating the
nationwide concept of
schools-within-a-school
using vertical teams. See
http://www.mpsaz.org/
redmtnranch/Vertical_
Team_Philosophy.html
for research findings on
this organizational
structure.

shared teacher planning and multigrade activities add richness to the curriculum. Students' individual needs are more easily met in this setting because materials for multiple grades are within reach, and the use of cross-grade grouping to meet individual needs is time efficient. The first day of school in a vertical-team neighborhood is a productive and comfortable day for both teachers and students as they return to a familiar environment.

The Daily Schedule: Middle and High School

Middle and high schools basically offer two scheduling options: an hour period for each subject area, or one of the configurations of block scheduling. The middle school schedule generally follows the high school schedule in order to prepare students for the high school experience.

The Carnegie Unit

The *hour* period schedule is based on the Carnegie Unit, a scheduling configuration that has influenced the overall organization of high school for decades. A Carnegie Unit is defined as

A measure of classroom attendance at the secondary school level. One unit represents one hour per day each academic year, or between 180 and 190 hours of classroom contact (United States Education Reference File, 1999).

James S. Frey, president of Educational Credential Evaluations, Inc., expands on this definition by describing the various ways secondary schools compute this annual unit of high school work. Although the *annual unit* is the most common reporting measure in the United States, some secondary schools use a *semester unit* to record a subject taught one hour per day, five days per week, for one semester (half of a school year); others use a *semester hour unit* to record a subject taught one hour per week for one semester. These three ways of reporting are related to each other as follows:

1 annual unit = 2 semester units = 10 semester hour units

Frey further notes that although the reporting is in units of an hour, that "hour" might be 60, 55, 50, 45, or 40 minutes, and the academic year might be 36, 37, 38, 39, or 40 weeks long. However, these inequities in time are generally ignored when curricula from two or more institutions are compared (United States Education Reference File, 1999). The criteria for receiving a high school diploma is based on the number of Carnegie Units earned on the required course of study. Although colleges and universities use the Carnegie Unit as part of their admission criteria, the inequity in class time that defines a Carnegie Unit makes it difficult for college admission officers to evaluate how much time an applicant has spent on required course work.

The Carnegie Unit has been criticized in recent years because of its emphasis on time spent in courses, the instructional organization of discrete 40-plus-minute segments, and the unit earned rather than emphasis on the knowledge acquired (Maeroff, 1994). Critics also say that the pace a typical student pursues in nine different locations doing nine different activities in a six-and-a-half-hour school day is grueling. The pace for the teacher is grueling as well: an average teacher teaches five classes each day, works with 125 to 180 students, and makes multiple daily preparations. As Carroll (1994) states, "It produces a hectic, impersonal, inefficient instructional environment; provides inadequate time for probing ideas in depth; and tends to discourage using a variety of learning activities." Individual students learn at differing rates and in different ways, yet the hour period allocates identical time for all students. In addition, lost time occurs during the multiple class changes and administrative duties that accompany starting and ending so many classes in one day. The Carnegie Unit is an organizational system that emphasizes an inflexible use of time that, for many students, does not serve their learning needs.

Block Scheduling

In response to the criticisms of the Carnegie Unit and the need for a longer instructional period than the hour period, the concept of block scheduling was introduced. Cawelti (1994) defines block scheduling as follows:

At least part of the daily schedule is organized into larger blocks of time (more than 60 minutes) to allow flexibility for a diversity of instructional activities.

The variations of block scheduling are many and may involve reconfiguring the lengths of terms as well as the daily schedule. Some possible variations include:

- Four 90-minute blocks per day; school year divided into two semesters; formerly yearlong courses completed in one semester
- Alternate-day block schedule: six or eight courses spread out over two days; teachers meet with half of their students each day
- Two large blocks and three standard-sized blocks per day: year divided into 60-day trimesters with a different subject taught in the large blocks each trimester
- Some classes (e.g., band, typing, foreign language) taught daily, others in longer blocks on alternate days

- Six courses, each meeting in three single periods, and one double period per week
- Seven courses, with teachers meeting with students three days out of four—twice in single periods, once in a double period (Canady & Rettig, 1995)

Regardless of the configuration of the block schedule, the most important issue is that it drastically changes the way instructional time is used and instruction is delivered. There is decreased reliance on the standard lecture-discussion-seatwork pattern and an increase in individualization and creative teaching strategies. These larger blocks of time allow for a more flexible classroom environment in which teachers can use more varied and interactive styles of teaching. Figures 2.1 and 2.2 are examples of two of the most frequently used block schedule configurations.

Figure 2.1
Four-Block Schedule

Monday–Friday

Block A
(85–90 minutes)

Activity Period
(30 minutes)

Block B
(85–90 minutes)

Lunch
(30 minutes)

Block C
(85–90 minutes)

Activity Period
(30 minutes)

Block D
(85–90 minutes)

On the surface, block scheduling seems to be the answer to some of the time problems inherent in the Carnegie Unit schedule. However, the process of making

Figure 2.2
Combination Schedule

Monday, Wednesday, and Friday: Seven 50-Minute Periods
Tuesday and Thursday: Four 80-Minute Blocks

Monday	Tuesday	Wednesday	Thursday	Friday
1st Period 50 minutes	1st Period 80 minutes	1st Period 50 minutes	1st Period 80 minutes	1st Period 50 minutes
2nd Period		2nd Period		2nd Period
	Activity Period 40 minutes		Activity Period 40 minutes	
3rd Period		3rd Period		3rd Period
4th Period	2nd Period	4th Period	2nd Period	4th Period
Lunch 30 minutes	Lunch 30 minutes	Lunch 30 minutes	Lunch 30 minutes	Lunch 30 minutes
5th Period	3rd Period	5th Period	3rd Period	5th Period
6th Period		6th Period		6th Period
7th Period	4th Period	7th Period	4th Period	7th Period

the change to block scheduling is a challenge. The Northwest Regional Educational Laboratory (1990) recommends two years of planning before implementation. Teachers who have taught in 35-minute to 50-minute blocks for years need time and training in order to develop the skills and strategies necessary to teach in large blocks of time. Teachers who are most successful in block scheduling plan lessons

Steve Krasner (2002) has compiled an extensive bibliography of resources on block scheduling and use of time in school at http://www.ctserc. org/library/actualbibs /BlockScheduling.pdf.

to include explanation, application, and synthesis. Most teachers have had little experience in the application and synthesis phases of a lesson. Another area in which teachers need in-depth training is in cooperative learning, community building, and team formation.

Implementing block scheduling is a time issue—one that must be carefully considered before the schedule change is actually made. Without consensus among the superintendent, school board, principals, teachers, students, and parents, the change is likely to be met with strong resistance. Building the support of all stakeholders takes time and requires many opportunities for all parties to learn about the proposed new schedule and discuss the ramifications of the change (Carroll, 1994). Teachers need time for professional development to help them implement a new schedule and develop their abilities to use instructional strategies appropriately in a longer time period. Scheduling plans must be carefully developed to ensure that each student is provided the time and the opportunity to complete the requirements for high school graduation. So although block scheduling offers an alternative to the Carnegie Unit schedule, implementing the change is not only a time issue but also an issue that touches at the very heart of the nature of high school.

Pacing the Year's Curriculum

Although teachers have little control over the mandated daily schedule or the curriculum, they do have control over how they allocate time to teach the standards and grade-level objectives. Teachers' responsibilities for pacing the year's curriculum involve two important elements: teaching key grade-level or course content to a depth that ensures that most students master that content—in other words, teaching a curriculum that favors depth over breadth rather than being an inch deep and a mile wide; and assessing the learning needs of each student and providing interventions to help students move along a continuum of learning experiences that allows them to achieve grade-level standards.

Instructional pacing is directly related to time allocation. Too many times, teachers reach the midpoint of the school year and realize that there is no way they can accomplish the year's work or even cover what's on the upcoming test. So, pacing must begin the first day of the new school year.

The following suggestions can help you make important decisions about pacing instruction:

- At the begining of the year, study the standards for each subject you teach. Identify the key content assessed on high-stakes tests, and determine ways that you can connect key ideas within the curriculum area or to another curriculum area to minimize teaching the same thing in two or three different units or subject areas.
- Mark dates on a calendar of special events, such as standardized and high-stakes test schedules, holidays, and other school events that are likely to either shorten instructional time or cause students' attention to be diverted from the instructional program.
- Schedule the major parts of your curriculum in time periods that allow for uninterrupted time and that work within the testing schedule. Build in extra time for content that you know is particularly difficult for students or that requires spaced review and practice to develop proficiency.
- Identify those areas of the curriculum you can develop using learning centers or other independent work that can be done outside of school. For example, developing students' abilities to measure and understand measurement concepts simply can't be done in a three-week unit, so you might develop the measurement standards and objectives by making them the topic of daily "sponge" activities supported by learning centers that provide practice.

Refer to your *pacing calendar* every week as you plan your lessons. Quickly finding that your pacing plan is either too ambitious for your students or that the pace of instruction is too slow buys time that you can spend on other topics, and can alert you to the need to assist students for whom the pacing is too rigorous. Accountability demands that we take a "macro" look at the curriculum at the beginning of the year and a "micro" look every week because time for learning is a key variable in student achievement. Instructional planning is key to successful classroom management.

Effective Use of Blocks of Time Within the Daily Schedule

Once your pacing plan is in place, you can think about how to use the instructional blocks of time allocated in the daily schedule. You can choose from several different instructional methodologies and can structure the time within an instructional block in a myriad of ways. However, planning successful instructional activities includes the sequence of events shown in Figure 2.3.

Pacing the curriculum for exceptional students with identified learning disabilities and for able learners is especially challenging in today's standards-based environment. Resources that provide information and assistance in meeting these students' needs are available through the Learning Disabilities Association and the Council for Exceptional Children. Information on flexible pacing techniques for use with able and gifted learners is available from the ERIC Clearinghouse on Disabilities (1989) and Gifted Education at http://ericec.org/digests/e464.html.

Figure 2.3
Planning Instructional Activities

Tasks	What the Teacher Does
Preparing and Distributing Materials	Plans ahead—checks that there are enough materials for each student. Duplicate materials that each student needs. For center work, prepares materials, decides on procedures for center use, and posts directions, rules, and the assignment; decides on student groups if necessary. *Estimate the number of minutes required for class setup—passing out materials, setting up group work areas, and getting students moved to their workstations.*
Introducing the Lesson	Determines the lesson objective; decides on a motivating, interactive way to introduce it; decides what product students are to produce, and the due date for that product. *Estimate the number of minutes required to introduce the lesson.*
Delivering Instruction	Decides on an instructional strategy—a teacher demonstration, lecture, whole-class discussion, debate, or other strategy. *Estimate the number of minutes needed for the instructional strategy.*
Assigning Work	Decides on the directions and the amount of time required for most students to complete the assignment. *Estimate the length of time you need to give students to work on the assignment. Determine whether the assignment must be turned in before the end of class or whether it is homework due at a future time.*
Closing the Lesson	Decides on a strategy for lesson closure. Plans to give a five-minute "stop work and cleanup" warning followed by a two-minute warning so students can give their full attention to the closure activity. *Plan to use the last three to five minutes to celebrate what students have learned, link the new learning to real life and prior learning, review students' responsibilities for completing the assignment, and develop anticipation for tomorrow's lesson.*

Now let's look at ways to use various instructional strategies within varying time-frames. One key factor in planning a lesson is to consider the attention span of your students. According to the 3M Meeting Network, the average attention span of an audience is 18 minutes—and this is for adults (Burmark, 2002). We know that young children generally have short attention spans. (To estimate the number of minutes of a child's attention span, add two to the child's age.) So, for children in the elementary grades, activities within a time period should vary to include a mix of listening, movement, hands-on experiences, and individual, partner, or group work. Even though middle and high school students should have longer attention spans, many students continue to have difficulty paying attention to a lecture for more than 10 minutes. On the other hand, some children can concentrate for extended periods of time on a project, game, computer activity, or book in which they are intensely interested. So, it is easy to understand why time management is crucial to successful learning experiences.

Planning Learning Experiences

For each learning experience, the time for each element of the lesson varies with the type of activity and the students' ages. Use of time and choice of instructional strategies are also based on the scheduled time for the learning experience. However, regardless of the length of time, successful lessons include the entire sequence of events shown in Figure 2.1 above. Time wasted getting materials and supplies at the beginning of the lesson sets a negative tone and encourages off-task behavior. Lectures and seatwork assignments that are too long and group work and hands-on activities that are too short fail to accomplish the learning objective. A hurried ending to the lesson leaves students without closure—one of the key elements important for permanent learning. It is also a critical time for teachers to assess which students accomplished the objective and which students need more time. The old adage "Time lost is never found" rings especially true in the classroom.

Organizing, Distributing, and Collecting Supplies and Student Work

The following time-management strategies can help you develop procedures for dealing with supplies and student work:

- Establish a procedure for organizing and distributing materials for lab or hands-on activities based on whether each student needs materials or whether groups of students share materials. Provide containers in which to organize and distribute materials for each group. Designate student assistants to assemble materials in the correct configuration before the scheduled time. (This practice is invaluable for finding out what supplies are missing, broken, or unusable *before* class begins.)
- Plan at least five minutes for distributing lab equipment or manipulatives. This time may be shortened as students become more familiar with the procedures.

- If lab or hands-on materials are new to students, spend a few minutes helping them understand what the materials are, how to use them, what safety precautions (if any) to follow, and what they are to do with the materials at the end of the class.
- For science experiments involving messy materials, such as sand, water, dirt, and other liquids, plan an *extra* five minutes for cleanup. Chaos results when students are moving in every direction to clean up real messes. Ask the custodian for a large garbage can for disposal of consumable materials.
- Use a system to collect completed student work. Effective techniques include locating a basket in an accessible place and having students place their work in the basket upon completion, or collecting papers in the seating order so that they can be quickly returned in the same order. It is usually best not to have students collect other students' assignments, as the opportunity for misbehavior is high when students handle one another's work. In addition, maintaining the confidentiality of student work is one of your key responsibilities.

Organizing for Group Work and Learning Center Work

The following suggestions are helpful for organizing group work and managing students working at learning centers:

- For group work, prepare a list of the members of each group and the location of the group's work area as part of your preplanning. Write the list on a transparency or the chalkboard, or duplicate it and give a copy to each student. (This technique saves times and eliminates answering the question, "Which group am I in?" 20 times in a row.)
- Scheduling students' time for computer activities and learning centers requires a systematic approach. One strategy is to use computer work as one of a group of learning centers. The whole class rotates through the centers according to an organized plan. In some classes, center work is scheduled one day of the week for a 35- to 60-minute period. Plan the center activities so that equal amounts of time are spent in each center, and there is adequate time to complete an activity or task. Develop a plan to ensure that all students rotate through each of the centers and that the number of students at a center at one time is acceptable. One technique for doing this is to design a "passport" that lists the centers in the order that each group of students must follow. For example, if you have four centers and students are allowed 20 to

30 minutes at each one, they can complete all four centers in two- to three-center sessions.

- If students are allowed access to the computer when they have free time, have them keep a log of their time and what activities they did. Because some students rush through their class work so they can spend time at the computer, this record is a helpful check on students' use of time.

- For older students who are allowed to choose group members to work on special projects, develop and teach a procedure for that process before the option is allowed. It has been our experience that this process can be extremely painful for students who are not well regarded by their peers or who have learning difficulties and are per- ceived to hamper the group's efforts. Therefore, it is probably best that choice be allowed only when the majority of the work is done outside of class and the assignment provides several different options, such as preparing multimedia presentations, writing and performing skits or plays, doing research projects, or building entries for various contests (science fairs, engineering competitions, and so forth). Clear criteria for grading is an absolute must for project work that involves multiple students and a significant commitment of time.

Monitoring Time Spent on Instructional Strategies

The following suggestions help you estimate how long you should plan for various types of instructional strategies:

- Allow adequate time for completion of the laboratory and hands-on activities. Estimate the time based on prior experience; if this is the first time you have done this particular activity, allocate a generous amount of time and then monitor to see if your estimate is reasonable. Allotting enough time to successfully complete the work but not enough for off-task behavior is tricky, but careful monitoring of actual time versus estimated time helps you plan time allocations for future hands-on experiences.

- Evaluate the time it takes for each instructional strategy you choose. If the strategy takes longer than your scheduled time, it is best not to attempt it. Some activities, such as complex science experiments, research projects, cooperative group assignments, and others, simply cannot be done in an hour period. These activities are ideal for block schedules or when you can arrange to have extra time.

- For periods of 60 to 90 minutes, use a variety of instructional strategies in order to maintain students' attention. Limit lectures to no more than 20 minutes for high school students and 15 minutes for middle school students. A successful lecture technique is to insert breaks for processing information. Use brief discussions among student partners or small groups or application activities that help students apply the information just presented. Another technique for refocusing students' attention is to have them stand up when you present a particularly important point or summary. A great memory builder is to simply remind students of the point that was made when they were standing up.

- Perhaps the most challenging instructional strategies are those involving cooperative, collaborative, and small-group activities. Using time wisely during those activities requires teaching the skills of group work, setting reasonable time constraints for completion of the group assignment, closely monitoring each group's progress, and constantly evaluating whether each student is accomplishing the assignment or whether only a few group members are actually doing the work while the others observe. Begin the year with group activities focused on learning social and time management skills. Then plan group activities that are more content focused. (For a discussion of various strategies for group work, see Section 3 of this book.)

- Assigning individual seatwork as a part of scheduled class time is an excellent way to monitor student progress and give you time to work with individual students who need additional assistance. Successful assignments are those that offer a comfortable challenge for which the student is adequately prepared and that can be completed in a reasonable period of time with a fairly high likelihood of success. An example of inappropriate seatwork would be assigning 4th graders a set of 25 long-division problems when they are first learning the procedure for dividing by a two-digit number. Frustration sets in, poor attitudes toward math develop, and students practice making the same mistake so many times that it becomes ingrained in their thinking.

- As students move up in the grades, assigning projects is a way to help them learn how to research, structure their time to complete a long-term assignment, and make oral and visual presentations to their peers. Successful project work is based on development of the organizational and research skills necessary to do quality work. One way to ensure that this happens is to develop a sequence of experiences over several years to build students' abilities. For example, beginning in 4th grade, teachers can assign a small project due in a week. Each day of the week, they can help students organize a sequence of steps that they must take to complete the work, find and use research sources, develop computer skills (if required), and prepare their presentations. In other words, the entire process is an instructional strategy. Over time, less and less support is provided; projects are done over longer periods of time; and requirements become increasingly stringent.

Summary

Effective time management is one of the skills necessary for success in school as well as in everyday life and in the work world. Students need time to practice, rehearse, review, apply, and connect new learning and relate it to their everyday lives. Teachers who effectively manage time give their students the best opportunity to learn and to develop personal habits that lead to wise use of time.

In Chapter 3, we examine ways to manage transitions, administrative tasks, and interruptions. Efficient use of time for these activities increases the amount of time for instructional activities.

3 Managing Administrative Tasks, Transitions, and Interruptions

Time is the most valuable thing a man can spend.
—Diogenes

An important part of making your day go smoothly is handling administrative tasks quickly and developing strategies for making transitions and interruptions as short and orderly as possible—even using them as *teachable moments*. These routines and procedures form the backbone of an efficiently run classroom and help students feel secure in your classroom.

Wong and Wong (1998) define a *procedure* as how you want something done and a *routine* as what students do automatically. A routine becomes a habit for the student. The teacher's goal is to explain, rehearse, and reinforce procedures until they become routines. Wong and Wong recommend that you teach only procedures necessary for the smooth opening of class the first few days of school and delay teaching other procedures until they are needed as part of an activity.

Daily Administrative Tasks

Daily administrative tasks are those noninstructional tasks—such as taking attendance, collecting student work, and preparing and organizing materials—that must be accomplished in order for the classroom to function smoothly. Developing routines to handle these tasks saves time. Implementing a system of student helpers also saves time and teaches students the real-life skill of accepting

responsibility for doing a job. The following procedures can be implemented at all grade levels:

- Decide on jobs that help classroom routines run smoothly
- Write job descriptions for each and job post them on a bulletin board.
- Write each student's name on a heavy piece of paper
- Post the names of the "Workers of the Week" beside their respective job descriptions
- Develop a system of rotation so that each student does each job at some time during the year

This system tells students who is responsible for each job, and the job descriptions remind students of their duties. Certainly, student-helper roles require more monitoring in the elementary grades, but middle and high school students can do these jobs independently.

Many administrative tasks occur at the beginning and end of each day for elementary school and of each class in middle and high schools. These are critical management times. Implement routines and procedures that create a welcoming environment and make students feel valued and comfortable. This environment is established the moment your students approach the entrance to your classroom—not just on the first day of school, but every day. Many students come to you shouldering incredible emotional burdens based on their out-of-school environments, relationships with peers, and learning abilities and disabilities. They look to you for warmth, guidance, and a safe harbor. Nothing is more important than reaching out to each student individually as he or she enters your classroom. Many times you can spot potential issues before they erupt into full-scale problems simply by observing the demeanor and attitude of students as they arrive. A well-organized beginning sends the message to students that you are prepared, that what they do is important, and that you value their time and your own. An orderly ending to the class or day sends students out of your class feeling positive about the day's experience and looking forward to tomorrow.

Taking Attendance

Taking attendance is a primary responsibility and should be done as soon as students are settled and engaged in the opening activity. Most states have laws governing school attendance and truancy, and it is your legal responsibility to adhere to those laws; for example, see the State of Wisconsin's Compulsory School Attendance and Truancy Laws, Memorandum 98-27 (1998). Figures 3.1 and 3.2 provide ideas for ways to take attendance in the primary and intermediate grades.

A teachable moment: Make student-helper jobs preparation for the work world by designing a simple form that you use once each grading period to evaluate students' levels of responsible performance.

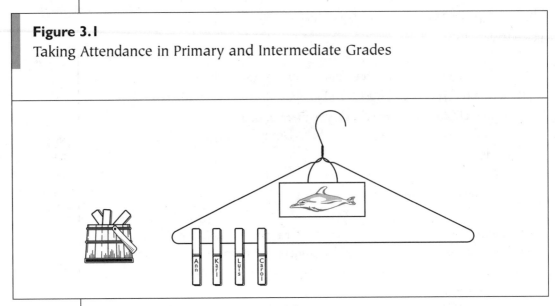

Figure 3.1

Taking Attendance in Primary and Intermediate Grades

Print students' names on wooden clothespins in indelible ink so that they won't smear or wear off. You can use strips of ribbon tacked to the bulletin board instead of clothes hangers. Put the clothespins in a small basket close to the pocket chart or ribbons. Label the clothes hanger or ribbons to identify various seating groups, such as table numbers or names. As children enter the classroom, have them pin their clothespins on the appropriate ribbon strips or clothes hangers. This system of taking attendance not only saves time, but also helps young learners recognize their names and their classmates' names and the name or number of their group.

The pocket chart in Figure 3.2 may be constructed using poster board and heavy paper pockets or cloth. Use stickers or a laundry-marking pen to print each student's name. Take a picture of each child or ask that they bring in or draw pictures of themselves. Older students might prefer to write their names on an index card and decorate it. Line up the students' pictures or cards along the bulletin board ledge beneath the pocket chart or put them in small baskets sorted according to their seating groups. Locate the chart near the entrance to the classroom and close to the floor so students can reach the pockets. As children enter, have them place their pictures in their pockets. Leftover pictures identify absent students.

If lunch count is a part of your attendance procedure, have older students decorate both sides of the card and write "yes" on one side and "no" on the other side to indicate their lunch choice. Have them place the card in the chart so that their choice is visible. The student helper then records the information.

In the middle and high school grades, it is best that teachers take attendance because most schools have a formal procedure for collecting and reporting attendance data for each class period. In today's environment of accountability, it is vital that you know whether students are present and that absentees are reported to the

Figure 3.2

Taking Attendance in Primary and Intermediate Grades

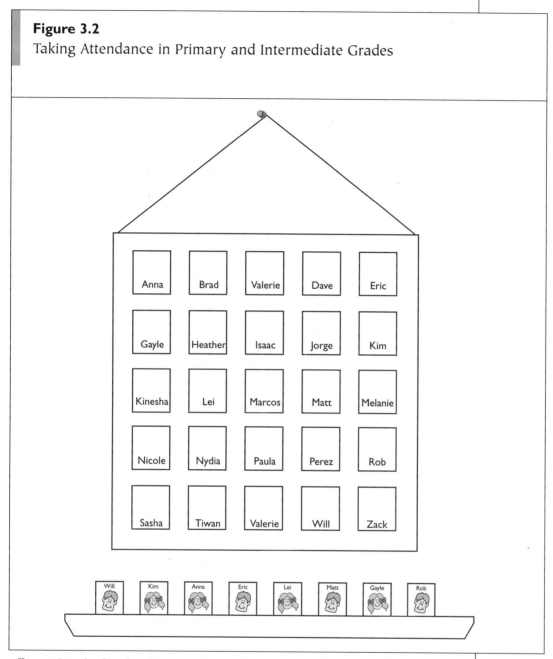

office within the first few minutes of class time. A seating chart is an efficient way to quickly glance around the room and identify which students are absent.

Another method that works well at these grade levels is to have an open file box or plastic milk crate with student work folders arranged in alphabetical order. As students enter the classroom, they pick up their folders. You can use the folders to return graded work to students and have them turn in work to be graded. Leftover

Do not group the pencil sharpener, the supply area, and the designated place to turn in homework and class work so close together that a crowd forms. Students clustered together trying to accomplish multiple tasks is a recipe for chaos.

folders identify absent students and also provide a place for the assignments and materials absentees need to make up their work. You can then quickly complete the attendance form. The end-of-class procedure includes replacing the folders in alphabetical order so that they are ready for the next class meeting.

Another important procedure to integrate with your attendance procedure is a plan for gathering assignments and class materials for absent students. One successful method is to designate a student helper to record the assignments, gather any materials required, and place them in a designated place. In some situations, making up all missed work is not possible. It is best to require students to make up critical assignments. You can provide assistance to students by arranging a brief meeting to review which makeup assignments are critical, setting a regular time that you will be available for help with instruction students have missed, and establishing a place where they turn in their work (Evertson, Emmer, Clements, & Worsham, 1994).

Beginning the Day or Class

A day or class that starts with disorganization and time wasted is one in which little is accomplished. Focus on developing and implementing strategies, such as the following, to ensure every day and class starts off on the right foot.

Give students time to store personal belongings in a designated place, gather supplies, sharpen pencils, and turn in homework, notes, and so forth. All these activities involve movement, so be sure that students can move about without crossing other students' paths multiple times.

Another strategy is to begin each day by welcoming the class. Briefly explain your learning objective and what students will do. Use this time to motivate students to participate in the lesson. Explain the purpose of the "getting started" activity and how it relates to the day's lesson or reviews material taught earlier. If students perceive the opening activity as busywork, you lose motivation before your class begins.

Carefully planned and implemented routines get your day or class off to a good start. Students feel welcome, and they are motivated and ready to learn.

Changing Activities

Changing activities within the classroom and moving to a special class or to lunch are times with a high potential for wasted time and behavior problems. On the other hand, these transitions give both students and teachers a short break and are valuable for providing a few minutes of downtime and some movement.

The key to a smooth transition is organization. Transitions work best in a three-part sequence:

1. Approximately three to five minutes before students change to a new activity, give a "stop and clean up" warning to give students a few minutes to finish what they are doing, record their homework assignment, and put away their materials. Have them return to their personal workspaces if they have been working in another area of the room.
2. When most students are in their assigned seats, give the signal for cleaning up the common areas of the room. Assigned student helpers should quickly perform their duties.
3. Give directions for moving to the next activity. If students are changing activities within the classroom, give them a few minutes to stand and stretch, gather needed supplies, or sharpen pencils.

Classroom Routines

Other important classroom routines include your policies for heading papers; dealing with incomplete, late, and missing assignments; and for student and teacher personal areas. Additional routines that require defined procedures include use of the restroom, drinking fountain, and pencil sharpener.

Paper Heading

Primary grade teachers are usually delighted if their students can write their own names on their papers, so a formal style for heading papers is usually not a high priority for these grades. However, it is good practice to require that children write both their first and last names (once they have developed that skill) and the date. The paper heading can be a part of the daily morning routine when students are learning how to read the calendar.

Elementary, middle, and high school teachers usually require first and last name, date, subject or period number, source of assignment, page number, and exercise numbers. The format you require for heading papers is a procedure to establish the first week of school. Post a sample of your required heading until students have established the habit of doing it correctly.

Incomplete, Late, and Missing Assignments

There is perhaps no other area of a teacher's job that is more frustrating than dealing with students who habitually fail to complete their work on time. This behavior is probably the topic of the majority of telephone calls and parent conferences because it seems that many times poor behavior and incomplete, late, and missing assignments go hand-in-hand.

The first step is to develop a policy that clearly spells out the consequences for incomplete and late work. Middle and high schools may have policies in place regarding this; if so, your policy should align with the overall school policy. Both

A teachable moment: Set a timer to help students focus on accomplishing the transition efficiently. When students are ready for the next activity, have them estimate the number of minutes you gave them to make a smooth transition. If students did not accomplish the transition within the specified time, hold a brief discussion to identify what happened, set a goal to improve the transition process, and continue to use the timer to help students estimate time. Building students' awareness of *about* how long it takes to accomplish certain tasks is a worthwhile real-life skill to practice.

It is good practice to immediately return incorrectly headed papers for correction, rather than grading the papers and writing a comment about the improper heading. If students know that their work is not acceptable unless the heading is done correctly, they are much more likely to follow the procedure.

the student and a parent should sign the policy so that there is no misunderstanding when students' grades reflect their poor work habits.

However, there are occasions when the issues of an individual must override policy. A student with a serious illness or home life that is temporarily in chaos should not be held to the policy, for instance. You can work out a reasonable plan to assist these students and make sure that they do not fall too far behind in their work. This relieves some of the student's stress and shows that you care about his or her situation. The policy is designed for students who exhibit a *pattern* of poor work and study habits. Have an open and honest discussion with a student to learn why he or she has developed poor work habits and to develop a plan for improvement. This puts the responsibility on the student to improve and puts the student on notice that you enforce your policy. Even though a student appears to understand the work, poor work and study habits can cause the student to make lower grades and eventually fall behind.

Policies for Student and Teacher Personal Areas

Students need a secure place to store their personal belongings. In the elementary grades, classrooms have a variety of storage spaces—individual student desks, groups of cubbyholes labeled for each student, lockers, and cloakrooms. In middle and high schools, students are usually assigned lockers. For legal protection, most schools have a written policy concerning the rights of school administrators to open and search students' personal spaces, particularly lockers.

Hold a class meeting to discuss guidelines for respecting classmates' personal belongings and understanding the rules that govern both student and teacher personal space. It is wise to make a rule that no one can put anything in or take anything out of a student's personal space. This eliminates the opportunity for a student to claim that he or she had permission to go into another person's personal space. You should define your personal space and tell students which areas are off limits. It is good practice to make your entire desk, including the desktop, off limits to students. That way there is no confusion as to what students may or may not touch. File cabinets and storage cabinets should also be covered by your policy. Some cabinets are accessible to students; others probably are not. During the first weeks of school, label the cabinets as "Student Supplies" and "Teacher Materials" so that students become familiar with the various spaces and the rules that govern them.

Use of the Restroom and Water Fountain

These areas can be recurring nightmares for teachers. It is probably best to tailor your policies to the age of your students. Primary students do best if restroom and water breaks are set at fairly frequent intervals. This allows students to move around and ensures that they have a scheduled trip to the restroom at a time when you are completely free to supervise. Help them understand that they should use the restroom at the scheduled times and try to wait until the next break. However, young children sometimes cannot go long periods without a break, so allow them to go without asking if the bathroom is located in the classroom and within your sight. If not, use a bathroom pass system. Have students put a small object at their assigned seat to indicate they are in the restroom. A real benefit of this procedure is that only one student can go at one time, eliminating the temptation to use a restroom break as "play time."

Intermediate grade students usually do well with a scheduled break in the morning, at lunch, and in the afternoon. A good policy is to allow free use of the restroom only during independent work time so students are not leaving the room during instructional activities. The use of a bathroom pass system is a good idea. Having two passes—one for the girls and one for the boys—ensures that only two students from your class are in the restrooms at any one time.

Because middle and high school students usually have time between classes to use the restroom and get a drink of water, this should not be a huge issue. Most schools require that students have a pass if they are in the halls during class time, so you can use the school's official pass form. Certainly, there are times when students *need* to use the restroom, but be alert to students who tend to abuse the privilege. This could indicate either a physical problem or other problematic behaviors.

Many students exhibit poor work habits as early as the primary grades. Even though they may not have a written policy, primary teachers should treat the issue seriously and work with students and parents to understand why problems are occurring and establish a home and school plan to help students improve.

The Pencil Sharpener

Thankfully, more and more students these days use mechanical pencils. However, the grinding of pencils is still an issue in many classrooms. The best policy is to set times when pencils may be sharpened. Unfortunately, pencil lead doesn't usually break at scheduled times. One survival strategy is to keep a cup of sharpened pencils by the pencil sharpener. When a student's pencil breaks, he or she puts the broken pencil in a box placed near the pencil sharpener and takes one from the cup. At a scheduled time, the student can return the borrowed pencil and sharpen the one he or she placed in the box. Keeping the cup of pencils sharpened can be one of the routine jobs of a student helper. Of course, you can always hope that students come to class with more than one sharp pencil.

Emergencies and Disaster Drills

Every school has a published procedure for reacting to emergencies and disasters such as fires, bomb threats, severe weather, and any other situation that requires complete evacuation of the building or moving to identified safe places inside the building. You should get a copy of this policy before students begin school.

See the references at the back of this book for information on policies for searches of student lockers developed by Avalon West School District (2003) and for South Portland High School.

For more information on crisis management and establishing crisis teams, see *How to Prepare for and Respond to a Crisis* (Schonfeld, Lichenstein, Pruett, & Speese-Linehan, 2002) and the resources provided by the National Resource Center for Safe Schools at http://www.safetyzone.org/home.html.

Drills to prepare students for a possible emergency should be taken as seriously as an actual emergency. We should never forget the heroic acts of teachers on September 11 who moved quickly and efficiently to ensure that their students were as safe as possible given the scope of the tragic events. I remember hearing a story reported on television about a 2nd grade teacher who taught in a school just a few blocks from the World Trade Center. When she realized the extent of the emergency, she listed the names of all students present that day, wrote a note on the list to let parents know where she planned to take the children, and posted the list on the front door of the school. She then walked her students to safety and stayed with them until the last child was reunited with his parents. Imagine the gratitude of those parents for that wonderful teacher's quick thinking in a time of crisis.

What are your responsibilities in an emergency? First and foremost, you must have an accurate list of the students in your class. Your grade book or class record book should be in an easily accessible place and should contain a schedule for students who routinely leave your classroom for special services, a daily schedule showing when your students are with another teacher, and a record of absentees.

Second, you should have a map posted in your classroom that shows the evacuation route from your classroom. Your responsibility is to see that the map is clearly visible and to review with students the route that they must follow. Elementary teachers should practice emergency drills two or three times during the first few weeks of school and define a standard lining-up procedure for all emergency drills. It is important that students quickly stand, push in their chairs if they are seated at tables, and move quickly to the line. Teachers should practice that procedure several times. Students must understand that you cannot use the daily lining-up procedure during emergencies because there is not enough time. Middle and high school teachers must take time during the first week of school to review school procedures, teach the evacuation route, and define an efficient lining-up procedure that students do automatically.

It is critical that students understand that the "rule of silence" begins the moment the alarm is sounded and ends only when they return safely to their classrooms. Explain that students must be silent in order to hear directions to change their evacuation route or to go to an area of the school property that is not their designated area.

If students must remain outside the building or away from their classrooms for a long period of time, it is important that they get good information about what is happening and that you involve them in some silent activity that keeps them from getting bored and restless. Stretching and alternating between sitting and standing help pass time. Assign an "exercise coach" to lead the activities. Changing coaches by pointing to a different student every few minutes keeps students alert and participating.

Emergency drills are critically important. One of your most important responsibilities is the safety of your students. Take the time to develop good procedures, practice them, and explain to students the importance of following the procedure.

Summary

The number of daily transitions, administrative tasks, and interruptions that teachers face is amazing. These events can waste an incredible amount of time and cause students to get off task. Time spent thinking through efficient ways to handle these events, teaching them during the first few weeks of school, and carefully monitoring students' performance pays handsome dividends for the remainder of the year. The time saved can be used to help individual students, allow students to complete more of their work in class rather than as homework, and provide a calm environment conducive to learning.

In Chapter 4, we will focus on ways to save teacher time when planning lessons, grading papers, providing feedback to students, and planning and holding parent conferences. All of these activities are critical to your success as a teacher and to the growth of your students.

4

Managing Teacher Time

Time is the coin of your life. Only you can determine how it will be spent.

—Carl Sandburg

Administrative demands on teachers' time have increased dramatically in the last few years. The proliferation of standards adds another layer of planning and gathering resources to teach these standards. In the meantime, the basic duties of teachers have not changed: preparing lesson plans, grading papers, and keeping parents informed of their child's progress. The time a teacher has for planning lessons and accomplishing administrative duties is never sufficient. In this chapter, we examine ways to efficiently plan lessons, grade student work and provide feedback, and schedule and hold parent conferences.

Planning Lessons

Planning lessons is your most important task. The best classroom management strategy is to plan an interesting lesson that meets all students' learning needs. When students feel they can be successful and that they are appropriately challenged, they find the classroom a good place to be. Transitions and routines fall easily into place, and time is well spent.

When preplanning at the beginning of the school year, set up a system for planning. These suggestions make the lesson planning process more time efficient:

- Make multiple computer labels for each course or grade-level standard. Stick a label in your lesson plan book to document the standards you are presently teaching. (Even if this is not required, the focus on accountability makes documentation a good idea.)
- Decide on a format for a lesson plan. If your school has a required format, consider making a form (or template on your computer) to meet your individual needs. Keep your plans in a loose-leaf binder or in a computer file so that you can track your students' progress from week to week. Note which students need adaptations to the lesson in order to succeed.
- Include your yearly pacing chart with your lesson plans so that you can refer to it weekly to determine what adjustments are necessary. Figure 4.1 shows information to include in your lesson plans.

The goal is to develop an outline to guide your thinking, not to spend a lot of time writing detailed plans. If you teach the same class or grade year after year, the binder or computer file serves as a reference to help you save time in future planning and to improve your practice based on past experience.

Your job is to help each of your students—each with varying needs, skills, and interests—accomplish the same required standards. Rose and Meyer (2002) present a practical, research-based framework called the Universal Design for Learning based on neuroscience research, effective use of digital media, and creation of flexible curriculum to help you respond to individual differences.

Figure 4.1
Lesson Planning Notes

Standard(s) labeled to show whether they are being introduced, taught, or reviewed (code with I, T, or R)
Instructional Strategies (such as those discussed in Section 3 of this book)
Materials including page numbers of textbooks, list of hands-on materials, and materials that must be duplicated for each student
Lesson Closure Strategy or Assessment Option such as class discussion to summarize and reflect on lesson, quiz, class assignment, teacher observation, and so forth
Homework assignment and due dates of projects or other long-term assignments (if appropriate)
Notes section to jot down the names of students who need more assistance or your comments about the lesson to guide planning for future lessons on this topic

I crafted many of my own lesson plans in my head as I drove to school. On my arrival, I immediately opened my binder and made brief notes to identify key questions to focus the lesson, instructional strategies, materials, and assignments. This helped me prepare materials in advance and focus on exactly what I wanted my students to do. At the end of each day, I spent a few minutes making notes to help me plan or adjust other lessons on this topic and to guide my planning for teaching the same topic next year.

Grading Student Work and Providing Feedback

Teachers spend many hours grading papers and recording grades. Many times we are frustrated when we observe students throwing away graded papers without even looking at them, much less taking time to correct their errors or ask for help. To make the best use of the time spent grading papers, first categorize the types of work students do and the purpose for each type as shown in Figure 4.2.

Next, decide your grading practices for each type of work product. There are not enough hours in the day for elementary, middle, and high school teachers to evaluate every piece of student work. Primary grade teachers can do this because most work is completed in class while the teacher monitors every child's work. Also, because much of the work in the primary grades is done using hands-on materials, working in centers, doing table activities, and participating in whole-group and circle activities, teachers collect observational data during these activities. So primary teachers spend their time preparing materials and observing children, rather than grading papers.

For elementary, middle, and high school teachers, grading student work consumes an incredible amount of time. They must decide how to spend that time wisely—grading enough of each student's work to make a valid judgment as to his or her progress and to determine a fair and accurate report card grade.

Based on many years' experience, I developed the following guidelines to evaluate the various categories of work products described in Figure 4.2.

Class Work

There are many forms of class work: individual seatwork, small-group work, learning center work, and so forth. The decision about whether to grade a piece of class work or to simply review it and mark errors is based on whether students have just been introduced to the topic or whether they have had enough experience for you to evaluate their progress or to expect proficient performance. If the work is done in groups, monitoring the group work informally is usually sufficient to determine how students are doing. If students have reached a point in the learning where you need to know each individual's level of proficiency, grading an individual work piece is important.

The value of class work is that it allows you to monitor individual students' progress and intervene before they fail an important test or become frustrated and cease to try. Monitoring students' class work is also helpful in making adjustments to your teaching strategies and to your future lesson plans.

Sometimes it is much more informative to walk around and engage students in conversation and look at what they are doing than to collect and grade a finished piece of work. It is easier to correct errors on the spot than to find the time later to reteach something. Taking a few minutes at the end of class time to discuss the

Figure 4.2
Student Work Products

Type of Product	Student Purpose	Teacher Purpose
Class Work	Practice or apply concept or skill in individual or group settings	Monitor students' performance, provide individual help, and plan follow-up lessons and activities
Homework	Practice for proficiency or apply new learning in a real-world situation	Provide additional time outside of class to achieve proficiency or to make learning relevant
Projects	Develop research skills, strategic skills for completing long-term assignments, a deeper knowledge of content, and the ability to make various types of presentations	Develop students' abilities to do research and broaden content knowledge, work in small group settings, develop skills to manage long-term assignments; make presentations using a variety of formats, and engage each student's interests and talents
Essays and Reports	Develop and practice writing skills, develop the ability to structure an interesting piece of writing that demonstrates what students are learning, how they think, and what they are interested in	Develop students' abilities to organize information, present it in an interesting way, apply skills of good writing, and show knowledge of a topic
Quizzes	Show the progress they are making toward a learning goal	Monitor individual student progress, determine areas of content on which students need more time, and plan follow-up lessons and individual assistance
Tests	Show accomplishment of standards and learning objectives	Determine level of student achievement on given standards or objectives; make decisions about individual assistance and next steps in lesson planning

assignment, provide some feedback to students about what you observed, and have them evaluate their own work is a more productive use of your time.

Homework

The topic of homework sparks strong feelings in teachers, students, and parents. The most helpful thing you can do is to develop a rationale for homework and share it with students and parents in a written newsletter during the first few

Marzano (2000) presents an extensive review of grading research and theory. Particularly helpful are rubrics for evaluating not only student work on information-, skill-, or process-based topics, but also on thinking and reasoning skills, communication skills, and nonachievement factors such as participation, behavior, and attendance.

weeks of school. (It is a good policy to send two copies and ask that one be signed and returned to indicate that the parents have read the rationale.) My rationale is that homework is assigned to help students develop proficiency on a skill through practice, understand a concept better by reading or studying, do research and develop a presentation, or apply what they are learning to everyday situations and events. In brief, homework supports personal learning. It is not something arbitrarily assigned because students must do some work at home.

Explain that it is impossible for you to grade every homework assignment, but that you know whether students did their homework and how well they did it when you grade quizzes, tests, projects, essays, and reports.

The following are some strategies for dealing with homework:

- Always tell students what the objective for the homework is. If students understand the learning purpose, they are more likely to do the assignment than if they view it as busywork. Try to make the objective relevant to students' lives. For example, if students are studying a world region, connect what they are learning to events presently happening in that region and to the importance of learning about other regions of the world. Have students find an article in the newspaper or record something from a television news program about the region. Then engage students in a discussion about what they learned the following day. Ask them to put their work on their desks so that you can quickly review it sometime during the class period or later in the day. I usually recorded a check, minus, or plus in my grade book to indicate the quality of the work.

- Check homework by asking students to demonstrate what they learned or did rather than checking each individual paper. Begin class with a brief discussion of the homework assignment or by linking the opening activity to the homework. Have students take notes on their homework papers during the discussion. Ask them to evaluate their own effort and accomplishment by writing a few sentences to describe what they learned. Have students leave their homework papers on their desks so that you can look at them. Record a mark in your grade book to indicate completion and quality of the work. I did not do this for every homework assignment, but chose to do it on assignments that gave me good information about student progress.

- Choose three to five questions or problems that represent the range of skills students must achieve. Collect the homework and check only the selected questions or problems. Return the papers and begin class by using the selected questions or problems as discussion prompts. Allow students to check the rest of their homework by putting the answers on a transparency or on the chalkboard, or by providing a copy of the answer key.

- Have students graph their homework progress. Assign the same number of problems, questions, or exercises each night. Have students make a bar graph outline on which to record their progress. For example, if you are working on multiplication in grades 3, 4, or 5, assign 10 problems each night, Monday through Thursday. Discuss five problems you chose as representative of the various types of problems and then give them the answers to the other five. Have them graph the number of correct answers each day as shown in Figure 4.3. Students in upper elementary grades and middle and high school can make double bar graphs showing the number of assigned exercises on one bar and their number of correct exercises on the other. This is a personal record of their accomplishment and clearly shows when they failed to complete their homework. Collect the graphs and keep them in students' work folders to share with students and their parents in conferences.

Help students understand that homework is preparation and rehearsal, not a final product. However, *never* assign homework unless you make it a part of what you do in class. If students do not feel that you value their efforts or that homework counts, their attitudes suffer, and completion rate is low.

Figure 4.3
Sample Student Progress Graph

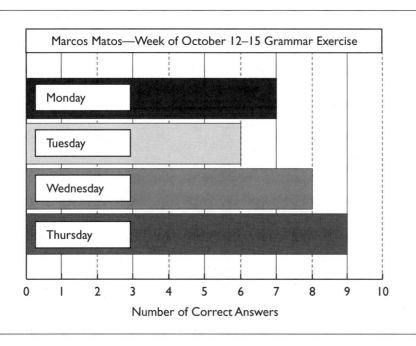

Marcos Matos—Week of October 12–15 Grammar Exercise

Number of Correct Answers

A teachable moment:
Ask students to record
at the top of their
papers an estimate of
how long they think the
assignment will take and
then record the actual
time it took them to
complete it. This gives
you a good idea of an
average time required
by your students and
identifies those who
need help either in
understanding the con-
tent or with time man-
agement skills. It also
helps you make deci-
sions about future
assignments.

Homework assignments that enhance learning and make it relevant are valuable. Help your students understand that homework is for their benefit, not yours.

Projects

As students move through the grades, expectations for completing long-term projects increase. Finding time during class to do some work on projects and expecting students to complete a good part of the work outside of class is very difficult when students have not learned these skills over time. The following strategies help develop skills and evaluate students' projects:

- Develop a curriculum across several grades for teaching strategic activities essential for success—time management, planning, research skills, computer skills, writing skills, presentation skills, and so forth. Work with faculty members to develop a plan that requires more independent work on projects each year. Make a time line for each project, giving benchmark dates by which certain activities should be completed. In the early stages of development, putting the time line on the chalkboard and highlighting where on the time line students should be help structure students' work. Gradually increase the time frame to complete the project and the expected level of performance and decrease your involvement in every step of students' work. This is good preparation for the work world.
- Develop a project-specific rubric. Students are much more likely to be successful if they know exactly what they are expected to do and have a rubric to guide their work. Figure 4.4 is an example of a four-point rubric suitable for evaluating middle school students' geography projects.
- If the project is a group effort, develop a grading policy that is fair to every member. One way to accomplish this is to make each student in the group responsible for a portion of the research, writing, and presentation. The group should present its work plan to the teacher for approval before beginning work. Another effective strategy is to have students present their projects to their parents in a special-events evening. Because this helps parents see the range in the quality of the work and how their child's work relates to other students' work, parents are much more likely to understand their children's individual grades.

Because projects consume large amounts of students' time, assign ones that help students develop competency on multiple standards and that make learning relevant and interesting. Don't assign a project unless it truly enhances your

Figure 4.4
Project-Specific Rubric: Grades 6–8

The Task: Research the geological characteristics of mountains. Compare and contrast the identified types of mountains. Choose one mountain range and describe its geological and geographical characteristics. Use models or diagrams, maps, and a report to organize your findings. Prepare an oral presentation deliver to the class.

Scale	Performance Indicators
4: Full Accomplishment	**Content:** Three types of mountains are correctly defined; comparisons show understanding of the formation process; information is accurately applied to the mountain range chosen. **Presentation:** Models or diagrams are accurate and neatly done; report is organized, comprehensive, and interesting; there are few errors in grammar and punctuation; oral presentation is well-organized and interesting; presenter makes good use of visuals; presentation style engages audience.
3: Substantial Accomplishment	**Content:** Three types of mountains are defined; comparisons show basic understanding of formation process but lack some depth; information is accurately applied to the mountain range chosen but some information is missing. **Presentation:** Models or diagrams are accurate but do not contain all required information or could be neater; report is organized and interesting but lacks some information; there are a few errors in grammar and punctuation; oral presentation is well-organized and somewhat interesting; presenter makes adequate use of visuals; presentation style engages audience most of the time.
2: Partial Accomplishment	**Content:** Three types of mountains are not completely defined; comparisons show basic understanding of formation process but do not adequately cover the three types; information is applied to the mountain range chosen but some key information is missing. **Presentation:** Models or diagrams lack key information and are not neatly done; report is not well-organized, and some information is missing; there are several errors in grammar and punctuation; oral presentation lacks organization and does not engage the audience; presenter does not make adequate use of visuals.
1: Little Accomplishment	**Content:** At least one definition is missing; comparisons are weak and do not show basic understanding of formation process; information is not adequately applied to the mountain range chosen and some key information is missing. **Presentation:** Models or diagrams are incomplete or missing and are not neatly done; report is not organized, and substantial information is missing; there are many errors in grammar and punctuation; oral presentation lacks organization, content depth, and does not engage the audience; use of visuals is poor.

instructional program and develops critical work habits and social skills. Time is too valuable to spend on an activity that does not yield a significant learning gain.

Essays and Reports

Grading reports and essays is another time-intensive task. Yet the only way to develop students' writing abilities is to engage them in the writing process and provide feedback from the inception of an idea to the completed writing. The most helpful thing you can do is to develop criteria for evaluating each writing assignment. Consider these questions and some possible responses as you develop the criteria for each writing activity:

1. What is the most important purpose for this writing assignment?
- Showing understanding of course content
- Organizing content
- Using correct mechanics: grammar, spelling, punctuation, and sentence structure
- Addressing a defined audience
- Engaging, informing, convincing, or entertaining the audience

2. How can I help students understand the assignment and my level of expectation?
- Develop a rubric based on each writing assignment. Students need to know your criteria for grading and the emphasis placed on each criteria. For example, if current instruction focuses on use of quotation marks, you may elect to focus your evaluation on that particular area of mechanics rather than marking every error. On the other hand, if your focus is on the organization of a piece of writing, you may elect to evaluate only that aspect of the paper and simply make a note to the student about the quality of the mechanics and other aspects of the writing. For students in grades 3 and 4, I found it more helpful to focus my evaluation on one or two criteria and did not attempt to give feedback on every aspect of the writing. Lynell Burmark (2002), who taught French in high school, elected to mark every error up to the tenth one. At that point, she drew a line, stopped grading, and returned the paper for correction. Her point was that it was not an efficient use of her time to continue marking errors on a carelessly done paper. Her technique worked—the quality of students' work did improve. The key is to know what is most helpful for your students.
- Share your evaluation procedure and rationale with your students. Encourage multiple drafts and careful attention to the mechanics of the

writing. Encourage students to read their own work aloud—it is amazing what we hear as opposed to what we see on the paper. A good proofreading technique for handwritten work is to place a ruler under each written line, look at each individual word in a sentence, and then read that sentence aloud. If students are allowed to use the computer, insist that they use the spelling and grammar check programs.

- Share excellent, average, and poor writing examples with the class and critique them in a discussion. (If you elect to use the papers of students who were in your classes in prior years, it is good practice to not only delete all references to the writer, but also to avoid passing out copies to each student. You never know when a former student's paper will fall into the hands of a younger sibling.) Make overhead transparencies of the examples and work either as a whole class or in cooperative groups to proofread the example. If you use cooperative groups, put the example on a transparency. Have each group work directly on the transparency and then share its work with the whole class. Collect the transparencies.

- Develop a way for students to share writings-in-progress with peers. Agree on the rules for giving constructive criticism, and give students specific things to critique on a given assignment. Provide time for students to read a draft of their paper to a small group or the whole class and ask for constructive feedback. This should be voluntary—some students do not want to share their writing in a group and should not be required to do so. Encourage students to post their work and ask for written critiques.

3. How will I give feedback and grades to students?
- Individual student conferences
- Written feedback on drafts of the writing
- Letter grade upon completion

We make subjective judgments on many aspects of students' writing. We can accurately grade the mechanics of the writing and react logically to its organization and the accuracy of its content. However, it is more difficult to judge the affective aspects of the writing—how it addresses the audience and whether it is effective in informing, convincing, or entertaining its audience. What is important, though, is that you maintain an open dialogue with students both in conferences and through written critiques that help students show growth in their writing abilities. Guiding students to understand the purpose for an assignment, developing their writing skills, emphasizing the various aspects of writing over time, and evaluating their

Grade the whole class's response to each question one question at a time. This allows you to keep in mind the key points required for an acceptable answer. Record the number of points scored for each question, such as 6/10 or +6 (for 6 points out of a possible 10). I was able to grade a set of papers much more quickly by focusing on only one question at a time, and I was less likely to know whose paper I was grading, which made the process more impartial.

writing objectively and in consultation with the student builds a strong writing program in your classroom.

Quizzes and Tests

Quizzes and tests determine student achievement. The difference is in the weight of the grade given and the content covered. The types of questions vary based on the content studied. Generally speaking, short-answer questions can be multiple choice, short answer, true/false, matching, or fill-in-the-blank, and long-answer questions require responses in the form of sentences, paragraphs, essays, and diagrams.

Short-answer tests can be machine-scored or graded by the teacher. These tests take less time to administer as well as to grade. Long-answer tests are much more difficult to grade, take more class time, and involve subjective evaluation. The following techniques make grading more efficient:

- Take a short-answer test before you give it to students and use your test as the key. This allows you to spot errors and questions that may not align with your teaching and to prepare a grading key at the same time.
- For long-answer tests, determine the point value for each question and show it at the end of each question. Write down the major points students should include in each answer before you give the test to spot possible problems in the questions. Have students write only on the front side of the paper and, if possible, put only one answer per page.

Quizzes and tests are two important ways to get report card grades. Plan to give enough quizzes to determine whether students are prepared for the final test. Spend time reviewing students' thinking processes—not just their answers—on the quizzes. Learning how to think and approach different types of questions is important preparation for the high-stakes tests.

Grading student work is one of the most difficult responsibilities teachers have. We want our students to do well, and many times we know that test results do not necessarily reflect what the student knows and can do. The best that we can do is to continue to monitor all students' progress, determine how they learn best, and present instruction in a variety of ways so that students have multiple pathways through which to learn. Give tests and quizzes in a variety of formats so that students become familiar with the various ways questions are asked and the various formats of tests. Then encourage your students to work carefully and thoughtfully on all their assignments. That is their best preparation for the test.

Parent Conferences

Time spent preparing for parent conferences is time well spent. You are less likely to get involved in long discussions about various issues if you have a clear purpose for the conference and have formulated suggested action steps. Strong partnerships with parents are vitally important to the progress of your students.

Use a *telephone log* to document and record your contacts with parents. Primary and elementary grade teachers might want to keep a Telephone Log Sheet for each student, and middle and high school teachers one for each class. Include the following information for each call:

- Name of student
- Person contacted and relationship to student
- Telephone number
- Purpose of the call
- Notes to document key issues discussed and agreements reached
- Next steps (include date of next phone contact or need for a conference)

Setting up conferences can be time intensive. The form in Figure 4.5 is useful for recording arrangements and ensuring that everyone involved has accurate information. If other school personnel need to be present, such as the guidance counselor, principal, or other teachers, the completed form should be shared with each attendee so they can include important information.

Parents are much more likely to become your advocates if they know you, understand your expectations, and feel that you are interested in their children's progress. Keeping accurate records of parent contacts is also important. If a student has problems severe enough to require consideration for special assistance, your anecdotal records and parent contacts become important documents.

Figure 4.5
Conference Arrangements

Name of Student	Name(s) of Parent(s)	Telephone Number
Date	Location	Time
Attendees	Date Contacted	Confirmation
Purpose of Conference		
Materials Needed		
Possible Action Steps		

The form in Figure 4.6 is one way to record the discussion and action steps agreed upon. It is extremely important to list the items discussed in the Notes section because it is helpful to refer to these records during later conferences to determine the student's progress or whether the agreed-upon action steps were effective. If the student is ultimately referred for special placement, these records document steps taken to assist the student prior to the referral and are helpful in defining areas of need.

Figure 4.6
Conference Record

Name of Student	Name(s) of Parent(s)	Date of Conference
Attendees		
Purpose of Conference		
Student Materials Shared		
Notes		
Action Steps		
Follow-Up		

It is a good idea to keep conference records in a secure place, such as a locked file cabinet where other private student data is stored. I kept my conference records in a loose-leaf binder stored in such a file cabinet. I organized the binder with the following tabs: Conference Arrangements, Scheduled Conferences, and Completed Conferences. In the Completed Conference section, I grouped multiple conference records for a student in chronological order, so that in future conferences I had ready access to earlier conference information.

Teachers who build partnerships with family members of their students are much more likely to understand their students better and meet their learning and social needs. All students benefit from being treated as individuals by teachers who truly have their interests at heart. Using part of your planning time to build these relationships is a wise investment.

Summary

A teacher's life can be defined by the adage, "too much to do and too little time in which to do it." The strategies, ideas, and techniques presented in this chapter are designed to help you make better use of the nonstudent contact time you have. It is very clear that when teachers have the time to make solid preparation for instruction, monitor each student's progress, and develop relationships with their students and their families, the classroom is a less stressful place for everyone. You have created an environment that allows you to be the instructional leader and students to learn in an atmosphere of comfort and calm.

Section Summary

Much of the content of Chapters 1–4 deals with your work "behind the scenes." This is important work that prepares you to be a strong instructional leader. A carefully planned physical environment enhances students' learning opportunities and supports them in being able to manage their own behavior. It allows you to use a variety of instructional strategies with the confidence that the physical arrangement of the classroom and the availability and organization of materials is sufficient to prevent lost time and off-task behavior.

Taking proactive steps to use your daily instructional time to your best advantage gives students a better opportunity to succeed academically. Addressing the issue of pacing a year's work before the year begins allows you to make adjustments in your instructional program before you fall too far behind, or to seek assistance from administrators when you realize that the required pace of the curriculum is simply not going to work for your students.

Planning ways to handle routine procedures efficiently and teaching students orderly ways to move from activity to activity within the classroom or from place to place in the building ensures that a minimum amount of instructional time is lost. Handling administrative tasks quickly and with the assistance of student helpers saves time and teaches students the value of accepting responsibility to accomplish assigned tasks.

Finding ways to save your own time so that you have more time to spend with students and to plan effective instructional strategies reduces your stress. Your classroom environment is more relaxed, and yet you are able to accomplish much more with your students. As each school year begins, make it a top priority to create a warm, welcoming, efficiently managed classroom. Your students may forget some of the day-to-day activities they did in your class, but they won't forget that your classroom was a good place to be.

Student Behavior

Jan Fisher

Exchanging Control for Influence

We believe that the intended modern school curriculum, which is designed to produce self-motivated active learners, is seriously undermined by classroom management policies that encourage, if not demand, simple obedience.
—McCaslin and Good (1992, p. 4)

Let's face it, the world is not what it once was. The technological developments of the past few decades have taken us from the industrial age to the information age with a speed that has left us gasping for breath. The new economy demands a different set of work skills and, along with it, a change in what is valued in the workplace: where the industrial age valued obedience, dedication, and persistence, the 21st century values innovation, initiative, individuality, and self-control. To prepare kids for these skills we must rethink teaching methods that are no longer effective.

Discipline in the 21st century should be proactive—focused on preventing conflicts and disruptions rather than on punishing misbehavior. We need to teach students responsibility, self-management, problem solving, and decision-making. The goal of discipline for today's students should be self-control; external control and compliance are not congruent with 21st-century values.

In Section Two, we will examine strategies for establishing and maintaining learning environments consistent with the new roles our students will assume. The strategies presented in the chapters that follow are based on creating a positive classroom climate (Chapter 5); establishing and teaching standards, rules, and procedures (Chapters 6 and 7); developing strategies that focus on preventing misbehavior and teaching self-control (Chapter 8); and, finally, developing a planned hierarchy of interventions that emphasizes teaching self-discipline rather than exacting retribution (Chapter 9). Taken together, these strategies represent a system of discipline based on responsibility, rather than punishment, that teaches students to be autonomous and self-regulated learners. The teacher's job is not to control, but to teach; not to command, but to influence.

—Jan Fisher

Classroom Climate

5

Don't you see my rainbow, teacher? Don't you see all the colors? I know that you're mad at me. I know that you said to color the cherries red and the leaves green. But, teacher, don't you see my rainbow? Don't you see all the colors? Don't you see me?
—Albert Cullum (1971, p. 36)

Who wants to cooperate with someone they don't like, respect, or trust? I don't, and it's probably a safe bet that I'm not alone. Most people prefer to work and socialize with people who are friendly, caring, and fair. Kids are no exception, especially when it comes to teachers. When asked to describe good teachers, students almost always say they are caring.

Establishing Positive Relationships with Students

Jere Brophy defines classroom management as "creating and maintaining a learning environment that supports instruction and increased student achievement" (1999, p. 43). The first step is to establish a positive classroom climate based on mutual trust, respect, and caring. The foundation of that climate is the relationships that are established between the teacher and students and among the students. Students like school better and have higher academic achievement when relationships are positive (Jones & Jones, 2000). Most teachers know this and try to establish some kind of connection with their students. This connection has become more central to effective teaching over time, and is the absolute bedrock of classroom management. Many kids come to us having never had a successful relationship with an adult. For some students, adults are people to fear and distrust;

others just aren't around adults very much. If we are ever going to positively influence students, we have to make a real effort to know them, and to have them know us, as people.

Students need and want teachers to be firm. The ability to blend firmness with warmth and caring is difficult, but certainly possible; firmness, warmth, and caring are not mutually exclusive. In fact, effective teaching involves blending these three ingredients together.

So, how do we go about making a connection and developing a warm relationship with our students? We must work diligently at this. The good news is there are effective strategies to do so.

Strategies for Building Caring Relationships

Model the Behavior We Want

Modeling is a powerful strategy. Think about the way children learn to walk, talk, and eat: they learn by watching adults. My granddaughter talks exactly like I do—same expressions, same tone of voice, same gestures. Did she get direct instruction? Of course not! She learned from watching me. Adults have an awesome responsibility in this arena because children do not only copy the wonderful things we do—unfortunately, they copy *everything* we do. Modeling needs to be done consciously and with precision and care.

We only emulate people we like and respect. If you want your modeling to have an effect on students, you must first build relationships with them. If they respect you and have a positive relationship with you, they will want to do what you do. As the relationship builds and deepens, the modeling has an even greater effect. This is a win-win situation.

You must model the behavior you want. If you want students to be polite, you be polite; if you want them to trust you, you trust them. Model commitment, promptness, enthusiasm for learning, active listening, anger control, consideration for others, honesty, and paying attention in an assembly. If you want kids to do something, you must do it first.

It is also possible to model unproductive behaviors. Do you have a messy desk? Are you late leaving the teachers' lounge after recess? Do you say things like, "I always hated math"? You don't unless you want your students to share your attitudes.

Modeling a behavior is not the only way to demonstrate how to do something. You can also model a process. This is known as the "think-aloud" strategy, and its purpose is to make thinking public. Examples include solving a problem out loud, demonstrating the steps you go through to make a decision, and verbalizing your thoughts when working to control your anger. Modeling product (the end behavior you want) or process (the steps of your thinking) reaps great rewards in terms of student behavior.

Establish Friendly But Appropriate Relationships

There are two major ways to establish appropriate relationships with students: by providing them with opportunites to know us as people, and by being open to their concerns and feelings.

Providing opportunities for students to know us as people. First we need to decide exactly how open and involved we wish to be with our kids. In their book *Comprehensive Classroom Management*, Vernon and Louise Jones (2000) describe three levels of openness for student-teacher relationships:

- **Complete openness:** teacher shares a wide range of personal concerns and values.
- **Openness related to school:** teacher shares feelings about school, but not about out-of-school life.
- **Role-bound relationship:** teacher shares no personal feelings or reactions but simply performs instructional duties.

All of us, but particularly beginning teachers, struggle with deciding on an appropriate degree of openness. Students respond best to adults who are comfortable with themselves, their beliefs, and their values, and who can share them nonjudgmentally. Sharing common interests—books, music, sports, entertainment—and discussing important ideas that are in the news, or that come up in the content areas, are good foundations for a relationship. Knowing just how open to be, and how much to disclose about yourself, is a matter of personal preference and professional judgment. We do not need to become overly involved in students' lives outside of school, but they need for us to be interested enough in them to share our ideas and engage in conversation (Jones & Jones, 2000).

Occasionally, teachers share too much personal information with their students. We need to be cautious about this; as the old saying has it, "familiarity breeds contempt." When a teacher discloses too many personal details, the line between teacher and student is blurred. We must maintain our role as "teacher." We are neither students' friends nor their parents. Our influence is most clearly felt when we act within our role as teachers.

Being open to students' concerns and feelings. Keep things in perspective; don't overreact to things students say to you. If a student says, "You're so mean!" or "You're unfair!" respond calmly, or with humor. Say something like, "You know, you may be right." We are the adults in these situations, and we need to model adult behavior. We can have a fit when the student says for the hundredth time, "I forgot my homework." Or, we can follow Fay and Funk's *Teaching with Love and Logic* (1995) and say, "Bummer. It must be frustrating to do your work and not get full credit. When do you think you'll be able to turn it in?" These kinds of reactions go a long way toward establishing relationships with students.

Strategies for Building Strong Relationships Systematically

In addition to the casual conversations described above, we also need to take more systematic steps to build relationships with our students. This is more difficult with some kids than with others. Students who have never had a successful personal relationship with an adult are not going to embrace your efforts on the first go-around. Trust is not a commodity they have experienced, and it will take a lot of "relationship building" before they are comfortable letting down their guards. The following strategies can help you succeed in this regard.

Make a Connection

Take specific steps to make a connection. Show an interest in students as people. Fay and Funk, in *Teaching with Love and Logic* (1995), talk about writing six "I've noticed . . ." statements for each student. For example, "I've noticed you wear a lot of blue." "I've noticed you like jazz." "I've noticed you enjoy mysteries." Put these statements on a card in a card file. Twice a week, in private, say one of your statements to the person for whom it belongs. Just say it—don't add, "and, that's great" or any other comment. Make your statement and walk away. The student should not feel that he or she needs to respond. After three weeks, when your six statements have been used, you will be well on your way to a relationship. You have demonstrated that you are interested in the student. This is the first step to making a connection. I have tried this, and so have others I know. It works!

Maintain a High Ratio of Positive to Negative Statements

It is human nature to notice misbehavior. We see things that need attention. The trick is to not respond every time we notice! Frequent negative remarks almost always cause students to dislike school. We tend to think that critical remarks improve behavior. Actually, research says the opposite is true. In classrooms where teachers make many negative statements, students perceive them as less understanding, caring, helpful, and fair. The message that students receive from these negative statements is that they are unworthy, incapable, and worthless. When this happens, students are not willing to work cooperatively with teachers (Jones & Jones, 2000). This does not mean we allow misbehavior to escalate. It does mean that we deal with it in more positive ways by teaching the students the appropriate behavior and giving them support and assistance as they make the change. Teachers who see misbehavior as a problem to be solved, rather than as a misbehavior to punish, build far better relationships with students.

Communicate High Expectations

Students like and trust teachers who believe in them and believe they can be successful both academically and socially. Communicating these beliefs is an important part of building a relationship. My 6th grade teacher was an expert at this. One day, he said to me, "You are an excellent cutter. Would you mind cutting some patterns out for me if you have time?" Now, I had never thought about my cutting skills one way or the other, but this teacher had just convinced me I had a future with scissors! He communicated a belief in my ability, and I was thrilled. To this day, whenever I pick up scissors, Mr. Howard's comment flashes through my head. It still makes me feel pretty good! To him, it was probably just an off-hand remark, but, to this 6th grader, it was the start of a great relationship. He believed I could do this important task, and that was certainly the way to build a relationship with me. Not many of us are close to people who consider us ineffective and incompetent! But, when they see us as skilled and successful, it is a different story.

We often respond differently to lower-achieving students. We give them fewer opportunities to respond, shorter time periods in which to respond, and less-specific feedback. Although we certainly do not do this intentionally, the fact is these behaviors do result in students feeling less valued.

Share Control

How many people like to be commanded? Not many that I know of, and I include myself. I like to have some say in what happens to me; control over one's life is something that everyone wants and needs. When we don't get it, we go after control over others. Because many of our discipline problems in school either start or end with a power struggle, it is a good idea to look at the idea of sharing control with the students.

One of the first books I ever read on management began with the statement, "The only behavior you can control is your own." That made sense to me! I thought about the people in my family whom I thought I could control—my husband, my children. Did they do everything I said? Not on your life! Even the poodle wasn't under my control. She would much rather just stand and wag her tail while I commanded her to "Sit!" I realized how I got around this problem. If I wanted my husband to do the grocery shopping, I did it by changing my behavior rather than trying to change his. I gave him a choice rather than a command: "I'll make lasagna if you'll do the grocery shopping this week." Saying "Do the shopping!" would not have worked; cutting a deal with the lasagna did.

Negotiate and Provide a Choice

Getting cooperation is easier and more effective than gaining control. How many years have we tried to make kids do their homework, finish their assignment, clean up their desk, and walk quietly? Too many! Let's think about changing our behavior in order to get them to change theirs. When we give choices, we give away some of our control. The good news is that the other person does not have to fight us for it.

Giving choices does not mean we put the student in control. I am talking here about structured choices—choices within limits. Fay and Funk, in *Teaching with Love and Logic* (1995), tell us that giving choices requires some limits, such as these:

- **Choices need to be authentic and legitimate.** The choice, "Do you want to do your work or miss recess?" doesn't give the kids much control, especially if this child lives for recess.
- **Both choices need to be acceptable to the teacher and the student getting them.** "Finish your work or stay in class for lunch" may not be acceptable to you if you miss your lunch when the student chooses to stay inside. Be sure you can live with either choice. Don't back yourself into a corner with a choice that doesn't work for you.
- **Say each of your choices with equal amounts of enthusiasm.** To emphasize the one *you* prefer in order to influence the student is manipulation.

There are endless numbers of situations where the teacher can give legitimate and authentic choices:

- Do you want to read before or after lunch?
- Would you rather clean up before or after we go to the library?
- Shall I call your mother or your father?
- Would you rather finish your assignment at recess or lunch?
- You can work alone or with a partner.
- Would you rather work here or at the back table?

Giving choices avoids power struggles and teaches students to make good decisions, and to assume responsibility for the outcomes-good or bad. Choices are essential for the development of student self—control, and they are discussed in each chapter of this section. When you provide the opportunity for choice, powerful messages are sent to kids (Fay & Funk, 1995):

- "You are in control of your behavior so you are responsible for it."
- "You are in control of making good choices within an acceptable limit."
- "You are competent to make these choices for yourself."

With these kinds of messages, the class climate becomes more pleasant. Stronger relationships with students result. When you let them know that they can, at least to some extent, control their own lives and that you respect their ability to do so, they begin to feel more valued and confident. The respect begins to be returned. You changed your behavior and caused students to change theirs. You gave up control, but you gained influence—and influence lasts forever!

Using Effective Communication Skills

Effective communication skills are as important in the classroom as they are in other aspects of our life. Actually, they are the foundation of good management. If we don't master the art of communication, our attempts to create a smooth management system and to build relationships with our students are limited. Caring interpersonal interactions are needed to meet students' needs for safety, security, belongingness, and self-esteem. Communication skills are divided into two categories: sending skills and receiving skills.

Sending Skills

These are the skills we use when we speak to others. Teachers use these skills in the following three ways:

- To confront students about skills they need to change
- To provide feedback to students
- To present positive expectations to students

The language we use with our students should be language that supports learning. In a 2002 seminar, "Improving Student Achievement Through Classroom Observations and Feedback," the New Teacher Center at the University of California, Santa Cruz, discussed strategies from the work of Costa and Garmston (1994) that support the learning of new teachers. These same strategies are equally effective in supporting the learning of our students:

- An approachable voice
- Acceptance, empathy

- Use of open-ended questions
- Use of present tense, such as "How do you usually get your anger under control?" rather than, "Why didn't you have your anger under control?"
- Use of positive presuppositions, such as "The student carefully thought through the issues under discussion," "The student acted with the most noble purpose that is possible in the current situation," or "The student acted with the best of intentions."
- Use of inquiries framed with tentativeness, such as
  - I'm curious about . . .
  - Would you tell me more about . . . ?
  - I'm not sure I understand . . .
  - I wonder what you mean by . . .

For further information on language that supports learning, please refer to Costa and Garmston's *Cognitive Coaching: A Foundation for Renaissance Schools* (1994).

Receiving Skills

These are, of course, listening skills. They are extremely important. When teachers use listening skills effectively, students feel significant, confident, respected, and responsible. When students are sharing problems, personal concerns, or emotions, the need for empathic and non-evaluative listening is apparent. Our job is to listen in an active way in order to help students identify the problem and work through it to a solution. Three important active listening strategies are clarifying, paraphrasing, and asking mediational questions.

Clarifying indicates that the listener has heard what the speaker said, but does not fully understand.

- Would you tell me a little more about . . . ?
- Let me see if I understand . . .
- I'd be interested in hearing more about . . .
- Would you give me an example . . . ?

Paraphrasing communicates that the listener heard, understands, and cares about what the speaker said.

- In other words . . .
- So . . .
- What I'm hearing then is . . .

- What I hear you saying is . . .

Mediational questions assist the student in analyzing what worked or didn't work and in hypothesizing or imagining possibilities.

- What's another way you might . . . ?
- What do you think would happen if . . . ?
- How did you decide . . . ?
- What would it look like to . . . ?

Building Community Among Students

Building a classroom community goes beyond the teacher-student relationship. It encompasses the broader idea of how everyone gets along together. Alfie Kohn (1996) suggests that the way students turn out is not just a function of what they have been taught, but of how their environment has been set up. We have to pay attention to the way the classroom works and behaves—to the structure of the classroom itself—not just the way individuals work and behave.

The quality of relationships that kids have with their peers affects both their academic achievement and their school behavior. Furthermore, the kinds of relationships that kids form at school are the basis for those they have as adults. It is in school, where students learn the social skills that assist both their social and emotional development.

We want our classrooms to be seen as communities of learners where all students are responsible for their own learning and also the learning of others. The foundation of this community is the development of peer relationships in which students show respect for each other and have concern for the learning, safety, and security of their classmates.

There are four major roles the teacher has in facilitating the relationships among students: planning activities, establishing group norms, teaching social skills, and focusing on cooperation.

Plan Activities

There are many activities, games, and lessons that teachers can plan for students so they will feel a sense of belonging. Activities for getting acquainted should be an important part of the first weeks of the school year. People, including students, are always more relaxed and comfortable working with those they know. In a community of learners, students interact with each other often, so setting up the conditions for that pays off in spades. There are many wonderful sources for activities that introduce students to one another and teach them how to work together in a cooperative and collaborative way. Some favorite "get acquainted" activities include the following:

- Have each student interview a classmate and then introduce that person to the class. The complexity of the interview can be adjusted to suit the age group of your class. Have students generate a list of questions that help them know classmates better. Write the questions on the board for students to use in their interviews.
- Prepare a Bingo-like grid with a question, statement, or characteristic in each square. Students walk around the room to find the person who matches the statement in the square. The person signs the square. The activity is over when each person has each square signed. Some examples for the grid include:
  - Classmate who lives on my street
  - Classmate who was born in the same month I was
  - Classmate whose favorite book is *Charlotte's Web*
  - Classmate who wears glasses

Statements in the square can be almost anything you want them to be. This activity is successful from age 6 to adult.

Establish Group Norms

Norms go beyond the rules and procedures associated with class management. Norms are the shared values of a classroom—the values we have as a group that help us to be a community. Establishing norms is the intersection of management and character education. Norms make the group strong and cohesive. High value on academic achievement is a group norm, as is valuing diversity and committing to make the room a safe place for all learners. Norms need to be developed, not mandated. A teacher can facilitate the development of positive norms by:

- **Labeling students' feelings and behaviors.** The teacher's question, "Did you see the look on John's face when you shared your lunch with him? Boy, was he happy," is the beginning of the norm that we help people out in order to make them feel good, not to make ourselves look good. The statements, "You must feel very good about the effort you put forth on your science project. It certainly deserved a blue ribbon," label the norm that effort pays off.

- **Modeling positive behaviors.** Modeling your enthusiasm for learning, your awe of people who have accomplished great things in the academic world, and your style of giving feedback, resolving problems, and finishing a task are powerful ways to get students to adopt these characteristics as norms for their group.
- **Integrating group norms with the curriculum.** This is an opportunity you won't want to turn down. In talking about conflict, ask students to name an example from history and one from the classroom. Asking the question, "Why is self-control so important in international politics?" really brings together the ideas of self-control in students' lives and the need for it elsewhere.

The opportunities for teaching character traits, emphasizing prosocial behavior, and establishing norms are endless within your own curricula. In fact, our goal is to align our curriculum to the goals of classroom management. We don't just teach responsibility every Friday at 9:00. We need to immerse children with positive models, and we can find them in all disciplines (Cummings, 2000).

Teach Social Skills

"These kids are continuously bickering," a teacher once said to me. "They do not know how to solve problems on the playground." Had she ever *taught* the children how to resolve conflict? Social skills—those skills that enable us to live in a community—must be taught. If I want students to use active listening techniques, then I teach them. If I want them to learn to compromise, I teach them. If I want them to eat politely in the cafeteria, then I teach them. I don't mean I *tell* them. I design lessons, and I model; they practice, and practice, and practice, and practice! I teach social skills just as I teach academic skills. Kids who are accepted by peers and feel a sense of belonging and confidence when they are with their age group are kids who are our highest academic achievers. Working in both areas is part of every teacher's job.

Focus on Cooperation

A community is cooperative, not competitive. It is a group of people—students and teacher, in our case—who share common goals and a common culture. Cooperation that fosters interdependence is the critical attribute of a community. We know that when we structure situations cooperatively, individuals support, help, encourage, and promote each other's successes. Structuring situations competitively results in individuals opposing each other's successes by blocking and obstructing them (Johnson & Johnson, 1984).

Structuring cooperative situations is one role of the teacher. Providing opportunities for students to work together on joint projects or in cooperative learning activities as frequently as possible assists the development of a strong learning community. To provide activities that lead to a norm of cooperation requires that interdependence be an attribute. Each person contributing to *one* part of a project, such as everyone adding points to meet a class goal, or every person reading and contributing to the total number of books read by a class, are examples of interdependence. Whole-class celebrations can be held when a class goal has been met. Cooperation that results in interdependence causes a group to be bonded and cohesive. It is an essential element of community.

*   *   *

I am a great believer in the power of a teacher in a student's life. We influence behavior and achievement in amazing ways, and making a personal connection with the students in our classrooms is where it all begins. For us as teachers, that same connection is what makes our jobs and our lives rewarding. The kid you remember from 20 years ago—you know, the one whose life you changed, and who changed yours—is the one with whom the relationship was strong. In fact, the relationship was everything!

6 Establishing Standards, Rules, and Procedures

Standards, rules, and procedures vary in different classrooms, but we don't find effectively managed classes operating without them.
—Evertson, Emmer, & Worsham (2000, p. 18)

When more than two people gather in one place—whether it is in a home or in a school—structure is needed. And the foundations of that structure are standards, rules, and procedures. In spite of the fact that most people agree with this, discussing rules and procedures generates feelings of ambivalence and nervousness on the part of many. Fred Jones, in *Positive Classroom Discipline* (1987, p. 42), discusses some very common misconceptions that persist. I have reprinted a few of them here, followed by my own responses.

- **"Students should know how to behave by this time."** They probably do know how to behave and have known since the 1st grade. But, they don't know what *you* will accept. They need to know where you draw the lines, and they will test the limits until you define them clearly.
- **"I can't take too much time to go over the rules because I have too much content to cover."** You can't afford to *not* take the time! The teachers with the most time on task and fewest discipline problems use the first three weeks of school to establish the structure so learning can take place.

- **"I announced the rules on the first day. I don't know why they aren't following them."** Announcing the rules won't do it. It requires teaching, modeling, and practicing for students to know what is expected of them.
- **"Teaching the rules is a matter of being strict."** This is not so! Teaching rules lays the groundwork for cooperation based on mutual sharing.
- **"Students dislike and resent classroom rules."** Students expect, appreciate, and respect a class with order. If your class has no order, you have a tyranny of the few against the many.
- **"If I have a lot of rules and procedures, the students won't like me."** The reality is quite the contrary. The most predictable characteristics of good disciplinarians are that they are relaxed, warm, and free from the struggle of establishing order.

The truth of the matter is students expect the teacher to be in charge. One student, a high school junior, said, "I appreciate teachers who don't let you slide, who make students do the work and don't accept excuses." Another high school student stated, "Teachers gain my respect by the way they control the class. They don't let students speak out of turn or give them passes to leave the classroom for frivolous reasons. They demand that students learn" (Boykin, 1997).

The point is that insufficient standards and procedures cause the loss of large amounts of students' time and interest. It is not possible to teach or to learn without order.

What Are the Standards, Rules, and Procedures?

Standards, rules, and procedures are different, but each of these is needed. They are used not to control students, but to teach them. Rules are not ends in and of themselves, but are the means to organize a class. Management decisions are driven by concerns about instruction, not concerns about control. A well-disciplined person is one who does the right thing without rules, and our goal is to teach self-discipline. Standards, rules, and procedures teach students what they need to learn to function successfully in a classroom community.

Standards

Academic standards tell us what all students should know and be able to do within each content area. In the same way, behavior standards, although not set by the various states but by the teachers themselves, tell us what all students should know and be able to do within the area of behavior management. They specify the responsibilities that students have to themselves, to their fellow students, to the classroom, and to the school. Behavioral standards define clearly the expectations that we have for our students in terms of skills in leadership, citizenship, independence, autonomy, initiative, cooperation, responsibility, and self-discipline. Behavioral standards are the support system for teaching and learning. They must be congruent with the content standards and the instructional models of the teacher.

Behavioral standards are expected norms for all students. They cover large sets of behaviors and do not change from day to day. Standards encompass all situations, and the good news is that they are relatively easy for teachers. Some possible standards include "Students are polite, prompt, and prepared" and "Students are respectful, responsible, and ready to learn."

Standards should be few in number: the fewer, the better. Three to five standards are about right. Some teachers limit it to one, such as "Be polite and helpful," or "Do only those things that help you and others to learn." These kinds of standards cover every imaginable situation. The students cannot find any loopholes! To make them operational, they must be carefully taught, modeled, and practiced.

Rules

Rules are absolute. They cannot be negotiated. They must be followed with precision. Rules are for safety and health issues, things about which there can be no argument. They, too, are relatively easy for teachers. Some examples of rules include:

- There must be absolute silence during a fire drill.
- Students must stand completely behind the line while waiting their turn to swing.
- In an earthquake drill, you must walk quickly and quietly to our place on the playground.

Procedures

Procedures are different. They are the accustomed way of getting things done. They are the routines that are necessary for the operation of the classroom. Procedures, unlike standards or rules, are limited to just one behavior, and they change according to need. Procedures are what make standards and rules operational. The bad news is that procedures are very difficult for teachers.

Procedures are difficult because there are simply so many of them. Virtually everything the students do in the class must have a procedure that is identified and taught. Every lesson has procedures built in, and if the teacher doesn't remember to teach them, the lesson can be lost forever. Ever try to pass out the paintbrushes and water pans for that wonderful watercolor art lesson you had planned without teaching the students exactly what to do with the brush and water? Either teach that lesson explicitly before you distribute the supplies or expect to have water everywhere but in the pan or on the brush.

There are hundreds of procedures: how to sharpen a pencil, how to head a paper, how to line up, how to carry the cafeteria tray, how to pass in the papers, but you can categorize all of them into six main groups. Figure 6.1 identifies these groups.

The key to developing effective procedures is to make sure you plan them for every routine in the classroom. Before school begins in the fall, make a list of every possible procedure that you think you might need and decide in advance exactly what you want students to do. This means everything from using the restroom and getting a drink of water to what you do if a student becomes ill or you have an emergency. Write down the steps of the procedure. This is very much a part of being proactive. It makes you ready for anything, and it lets the students know that you are ready for anything! When a child says, "I think I'm going to throw up," you will be able to calmly say, "Let me check my list. Oh, yes, it says 'send student immediately to the restroom, or if it is too late for that, remove all students from the classroom and call the custodian.'" This demonstrates to all that this teacher knows what he or she is doing!

When you plan lessons, don't overlook the procedures. Content and teaching strategies are important, but the procedures can make or break a lesson. You didn't remember until the middle of the lesson that you needed to divide the class into groups of four? You forgot that you were going to use the scissors and you aren't sure where they are? You didn't think of a good way to have students hand in their art projects that have wet paint? Think about the way you will handle all of these procedures within your lesson and include them in your lesson plan. Decide if the students already know how to do the procedure, or whether you will teach them the procedure before the lesson begins or when you come to it within the lesson. Do not leave any procedures to chance!

Guidelines for Effective Standards, Rules, and Procedures

The purpose for having standards, rules, and procedures is to teach students appropriate behavior. The first step is to establish them according to certain guidelines, so they will effectively teach students what the students need to learn without any negative side effects. There are three guidelines for establishing effective standards, rules, and procedures: They must be clear, reasonable, and enforceable.

Standards, Rules, and Procedures Must Be Clear

This is the most important *rule for establishing rules*. A rule must be stated so clearly and taught so well that those affected understand what behavior is expected. The major way to do this is by stating the rules positively, telling the

Figure 6.1
Categories of Procedures

Categories	Procedures for
Uses of room and school areas	• Students' desk and storage areas • Learning centers • Distribution, collection, and storage of materials • Teacher desk and storage areas • Drinking fountain, bathroom, and pencil sharpener • Office, library, cafeteria, and playground • Lining up
Beginning and ending of class or school	• Taking attendance and collecting homework and parent notes • Tardy and early-dismissal students • Sponge activities • Storage and distribution of materials
Whole-class and small-group instruction	• Interaction • Signaling for attention • Movement within the classroom • Materials
Transitions	• Time between subject areas or classes • Unexpected free time • Controlling noise levels and talking
Student work	• Paper headings • Incomplete, late, or missing assignments • Make-up assignments • Posting assignments • Collecting work • Due dates and times • Checking work (both students and teachers) • Turning in papers • Keeping track of what work is turned in and what isn't • Returning student work • What to do when finished • Getting help when the teacher is busy
Miscellaneous	• Disaster drills • Emergency situations (e.g., sick and injured students) • Movement around school grounds • Student housekeeping

Note: Adapted from "Classroom Procedures Checklist" by the American Federation of Teachers (n. d.).

students what *to* do, rather than what *not* to do. The rule "Don't run" does not help students know what they are supposed to do. There are many ways to get from one place to another without running. Hopping, skipping, jumping, and walking backwards are a few that come to mind. And, each of these will be considered and implemented by one student or another! If you want students to walk slowly, then your procedure is "Walk slowly." If you want them to walk quickly, then your procedure is "Walk quickly." You tell them explicitly what you want them to do. We cannot expect them to do what they cannot understand.

Clarity is one reason to state rules positively. Another is to avoid giving students any ideas that they do not already have. I am reminded here of the new teacher who had a fish bowl with fish and a rule to go with it, "Don't put foreign objects in the fish bowl." When I visited her classroom shortly after school began, she pointed to the fish bowl and said, "Look at this! The bowl is full of clips, rubber bands, pennies, and scraps of paper. I have the rule right over the bowl, but the students are just not following it." She was right. There were more foreign objects in that fish bowl than I had ever seen. The students had spent a good deal of time discussing what was and was not a "foreign object," and they had found a few that no one had thought of before. The teacher, with all good intentions, had given them some ideas that they didn't need. They were clearly focused on identifying and then dropping into the bowl as wide a variety of foreign objects as they could find.

The teacher and I discussed how to rephrase the rule so it more clearly expressed what she wanted. She came up with a perfect one, "Feed only fish food to the fish." It was very clear. Students knew exactly what *to* do rather than what *not* to do. A problem later emerged when the students fed so much fish food to the fish that many died. This time the teacher realized quite quickly that she needed to amend the previous rule and she did, "Feed one pinch of fish food to the fish." The problem was solved. Clarity is everything when it comes to standards, rules, and procedures!

Standards, Rules, and Procedures Must Be Reasonable

This guideline has the following four criteria:

- **The student must be able to do what you are asking him to do.**

  A standard that says, "Everyone will write in cursive writing," is not reasonable until every child can do it. If children cannot do what is required, then you teach it to them. Children cannot be held accountable for what they are unable to do.

- **A standard, rule, or procedure is unreasonable if you don't need it.**

  If only one child is eating the beans that you put out as counters in the math center, you do not need to establish and teach a rule to the class. It will only call attention to this activity, so others will try it. Sometimes, it is better to wait to see if you need a standard before you establish and teach it. We learned this the hard way when we had a procedure for going to the restroom. Once we taught this procedure, suddenly everyone was requesting the bathroom pass. After all, if the teacher has a procedure for something, then the students had better do it. We found that if the restroom was not mentioned publicly, but handled on a one-to-one basis of need, the bathroom problem was virtually eliminated. The significant learning here is if you have a rule for something, everyone will try it. You just might want to wait to see if a situation emerges that requires a procedure. If it doesn't, don't bring it up!

- **A standard, rule, or procedure must not run against human nature.**

  A rule that says, "Every child must sit up straight," is doomed to failure. This is a rule that seems to be attempting to change the basic nature of the child, something we probably don't want to engage in. Furthermore, there is no reason to have such a rule. Remember that standards, rules, and procedures should only be established because they help students learn better. There is no evidence that sitting up straight will do that. In fact, there is evidence from the learning styles research that many children learn better by lying on the floor (Carbo, Dunn, & Dunn, 1986)!

- **A standard, rule, or procedure must not take more resources than you can afford to use to enforce it.**

  If it takes every ounce of energy you have or half the minutes in a day to enforce, then the rule is not reasonable. I once had my students sitting in groups of four. It was difficult, if not impossible, for them to sit facing each other without giggling or being distracted by what their tablemates were doing or saying. I was spending most of the day trying to get their attention. It was wiser to rearrange the desks so they were not facing each other. The group sitting was not worth the time and energy it was taking! Kindergarten teachers often like their students to sit together on the rug. However, with some groups, the management of that is next to impossible. You have to ask yourself if sitting on the rug is worth the great deal of time it takes to implement and monitor behavior. You may decide it is not. When you have standards and procedures that require more resources of time or energy that are available to you, giving them up may be a very smart move.

Standards, Rules, or Procedures Must Be Enforceable

This basically means that the rulemaker can make it happen. If your standard states that "All students will be in their seats by 8:15 a.m.," but the bus doesn't arrive until 8:20 a.m., the standard is unenforceable. Get rid of it. A teacher who has a standard that every child shares his or her story with the class will have difficulty enforcing it on a very shy child. Good rulemakers know there are some things that cannot be enforced by standards, rules, or procedures, and so they avoid having such rules.

Another kind of standard that is hard to enforce is one that applies only part of the time. I often see a standard posted that states, "All students will raise their hands to speak." When the teacher begins the lesson, she says, "Now just think about this. Don't raise your hand. I will call on someone to respond." This is a great teaching strategy for getting involvement from all, but it directly violates the posted standard. This either confuses the kids or causes the teacher to lose credibility: "He has us do all kinds of things that go against the rules." Better to avoid having a standard that does not apply to *all* situations *all* the time. Figure 6.2 provides examples of standards developed by exemplary teachers.

Who Establishes the Standards, Rules, and Procedures?

This is a frequently asked question that probably has no one right answer. It makes sense that the students may be more willing to meet standards that they have had some voice in, but it is also true that all of us follow rules all of the time that we don't make. It is part of life. Still, I am more apt to follow a law to the letter where I see a real purpose in it, and I think students are the same. If the students don't actually make the standards, they, at least, need to be involved in a discussion about why the standards are necessary. As students discuss the purpose, they discuss the pros and cons, and in the process they construct their own meaning. Students, like the rest of us, are much more likely to meet a standard that has a good reason for its existence. Effective teachers establish standards, rules, and procedures in a variety of ways.

Liz Slezak, a teacher in Costa Mesa, California, tells students the standards she needs in order to make the class function well, and the students add any they think they need. Addie Gaines—formerly a kindergarten teacher and now a principal from Kirbyville, Missouri—involved her students in formulating the standards. She had them brainstorm a list of class rules, which she then placed on a chart color-coded according to common attributes. She asked the students to look at all the rules of a certain color and comment on their similarities. For example, if the

Figure 6.2
Standards from Exemplary Teachers

Share everything but germs.
—Addie Gaines (Kindergarten), Seneca, Missouri

* *I will be prepared for class.*
* *I will participate actively in the learning process.*
* *I will demonstrate a positive attitude.*
* *I will treat others politely and with respect.*
* *I will follow classroom and school procedures.*
  —Lisa Frase (Grade 4), Clear Creek Independent School District, Texas

* *Come to class prepared to work and with a sense of humor.*
* *Be nice to each other.*
* *It is NOT nice to throw things.*
* *Check the "forbidden word" wall in case your favorite is listed.*
* *Class is over when I dismiss you.*
* *In case of emergencies, hang on to the knot in the rope.*
  —Ann Price (Grades 10–12, History and Law), North Mason School District, Washington

CARE.
  —Judy Mazur (Grade 3), Walnut Creek, California

* *Be safe.*
* *Be respectful.*
* *Be a friend to everyone.*
  —Jennifer L. Matz (Grade 5), Williams Valley School District, Pennsylvania

Do only those things that help you and others to learn.
  —Liz Slezak (Grade 5), Costa Mesa, California

* *Be productive from bell to bell.*
* *Respect yourself and others.*
* *Listen during instruction and discussion.*
  —Tory Klementsen (Grades 9–12, Business and Technology), Marysville, Washington

* *You need not FEEL respect for everyone, but everyone in the classroom will be TREATED with respectful behavior and language.*
* *Your classmates and I take pride in a beautiful classroom. We appreciate your responsible treatment of supplies and equipment.*
* *Staff directives are to be followed immediately and accurately. If you do not understand, please ask. This rule keeps all of us feeling safe.*
  —Donna Coffeen (Grades 4–12), Walla Walla, Washington

rules written in blue included "no hitting," "no kicking," and "no biting," the students might conclude that the blue rules are about not hurting each other. Because Addie always wanted students to know what *to* do rather than what *not* to do, she might then ask, "If we are not hurting each other, what are we doing?" If the students were to respond, "Treating everyone nicely," they would have formulated a standard in doing so. Addie found such lessons to be very instructive for students because the lessons taught the students exactly what they needed to do (and not do) in order to treat everyone nicely.

On the other hand, one of the finest teachers I know, Jan Birney, a library-media center teacher in a Monroe, Connecticut, middle school, says, "Your standards, rules, and procedures should be set by you, the teacher, as you are the one who will guide your students to competency. So before you decide on any rules you will have in your class, sit down and think long and hard."

Some involvement of the students is important in establishing standards, but exactly how much and what kind is strictly up to the teacher. In terms of rules, because they are not negotiable and because they are health and safety issues, the teacher is responsible for making them. However, the students need to discuss the purpose for these rules and why they are essential. Procedures, too, are generally designed by the teacher, but students can offer great input in ways to make them more effective. When a teacher says, "The procedure I thought of for sharpening pencils is just not working. May I have your suggestions on ways to improve it?" students can have a discussion and generally provide some good ideas. Students also commit to the procedure because it was their plan and they want it to work! The teacher, at the very least, must have the final say even if the students do not agree. The fact that they have had their opinions listened to respectfully makes it likely that they will accept a standard even if it is not of their own choosing.

*   *   *

Establishing standards, rules, and procedures is just half of this important component of classroom management. In the next chapter, we will discuss the importance of explicitly teaching your expectations to your students.

7

Teaching Standards, Rules, and Procedures

You will begin teaching your classroom rules one way or another from the opening minute of the school year. Your choice is not whether rules will be taught but rather whether your rules will be taught.

—Fred Jones (1987, p. 46)

Fred Jones's quotation is exactly right. If you expect students to successfully meet your expectations, they need to know precisely what those expectations are. Standards, rules, and procedures may be taught in a variety of ways. One is by modeling your expectations. Picture yourself as a student on the first day of school. You arrive at the classroom door just as the bell rings. The teacher is busy sorting through papers at her desk. She motions you in, but barely looks up from her work. Everyone is trying to find the place where coats should be stored and where they should sit. There doesn't seem to be any kind of system, so some students throw their book bags in the corner and take a seat. Others just walk around looking at things, eventually dropping into a seat by a friend. The teacher is very preoccupied so you begin chatting with your friends. No books are in sight. Looks like this will be one easy year! This teacher's first standard has been taught: Come into class any way you want and begin to socialize.

Contrast that with a different teacher on the first day. You arrive at your classroom. The teacher is standing in the doorway and, as you arrive, he shakes your hand, introduces himself, and welcomes you to his class. He announces, "Your nametag is on your desk. Please put your things in the closet to your right, and find your desk. Paper and pencil are ready for you, and there are directions to follow on the board." Sure enough, there are instructions on the board! The teacher quickly takes the roll, while you finish your assignment, and then he is ready to go with a "getting to know you" activity. Looks like this will be a great year. This teacher has taught his first rule, too, but his message is quite different.

You have a good sense of the teacher's expectations already, and the school year is only five minutes old. You know where to put your coat; you have an assigned seat; you are expected to begin some kind of assignment right away; and you've learned there won't be a lot of wasted time. This teacher also cares about his students! He greeted each of you as you entered the classroom. The morning procedure is modeled and taught, and you have a clear idea of what your year with him will be. He has a structure in place, and you know what it is!

Why and When Do We Teach Standards, Rules, and Procedures?

Teaching standards, rules, and procedures is the most important aspect of classroom management. It is also the most frequently overlooked. Kids are not mind readers. They want to do well in school, and they want to meet the behavior standards in the classroom. To do that, they must know more than *what* the standards are. They must be taught *how* to meet them. They need to see the appropriate behaviors modeled, to practice the behaviors, and to receive feedback on their performance. Management is an established structure that allows learning to occur. Either you teach that structure, or you abdicate it (Jones, 1987).

Effective teachers spend the first two to three weeks teaching the structure. Of course, the students have work to do, but *your* objective is to get the management system in place. They may be doing math, but you will be teaching how to head a paper. Your instruction, questions, and feedback are all about heading the paper, not about math.

You teach standards as you establish them. You teach procedures as needed. When it is time to leave the room for recess on the first day, you teach recess procedures. When it is time for the cafeteria at lunch, you teach cafeteria procedures. As Jones says, "the willingness and capacity of the teacher to prevent discipline problems proactively through structure will determine how many discipline problems will need to be remedied reactively after they've occurred" (Jones, 1987, p. 49).

How Do We Teach Standards?

Standards are very broad because they must be generalized to all situations. They consist of many behaviors and procedures. In order to make them operational, a great deal of teaching is required. One way of doing this is through specific feedback, especially by labeling behaviors that meet the standards. If being polite is a standard, then every time the students are polite, you label it. Statements such as "When you pushed your chair in so nobody would trip over it, you were polite," or, "When you remembered to walk behind the speaker instead of in front of him, you were behaving politely," give students information they need about politeness. For standards that have so many components, this specific feedback on instances of the behavior that you observe is often the best way to ensure appropriate behavior. Given enough specific examples, the students begin to generalize about the kind of behaviors that make up the quality of "politeness."

You also teach standards explicitly using many different activities. When teaching students to be polite, have them identify examples of polite and impolite behavior at school and at home, role-play polite and impolite, write about politeness, or make a class book of different ways to be polite. The key is: If you want students to be polite, you must teach them!

How Do We Teach Rules and Procedures?

Rules are absolute; they are not negotiated. They are generally for issues of health and safety. Rules are often broken down into procedures to make them operational. Procedures are specific and apply to just one situation. The process for teaching rules and procedures requires the same four steps:

- **Step 1. Identify a need and write an objective.** In terms of procedures, especially, you teach *what* is needed *when* it is needed. If, on the first day of school, you open the door and the students are standing in a straight quiet line, you can discard the carefully planned lesson you designed for lining up. They don't need it. On the other hand, if they are milling around and talking loudly, you make a mental note to begin getting ready for recess 20 minutes early so you can teach, model, and practice lining up. You will undoubtedly have several lessons already planned and ready to go the first week, but if you don't, once a need is identified, write a specific learning objective and then plan and teach the lesson so students meet it.

- **Step 2. Break down the task into component parts.** This is an important part of most lessons in content areas and behavior. The task needs to be broken down into the teachable parts. For lining up, the sub-objectives might be to teach

  1. Walking to the line.
  2. Standing one behind the other.
  3. Standing an arm's length apart.
  4. Keeping arms at sides.
  5. Waiting quietly until everyone is ready to go.

- **Step 3. Plan the lesson.** The lesson in behavior should be as carefully planned as any lesson you teach. The elements of instruction that you feel are important for your class should be included. Figure 7.1 lists and describes each of the elements that may be included in a lesson.

Figure 7.1
Elements of an Effective Lesson

Anticipatory set	Accesses prior knowledge or experience that helps students to master new learning.
Objective	What students should know and be able to do by the end of the lesson. Should be stated in students' terms.
*Purpose**	What the lesson has to offer students, not the teacher. This is the "sales pitch."
*Input**	Information the students need to understand and perform the task. Teacher must be sure to provide all essential information.
*Modeling**	Teacher's demonstration and verbal description of expected behavior. Includes labeling of critical attributes of the behavior so that students have no doubt about which ones are essential to mastery.
*Check for understanding**	Allows the teacher to be sure students heard the information and understand what to do.
*Guided practice**	Practice under the direction of the teacher, who gives feedback on performance.
Closure	Student summary of the steps of the procedure or the main idea of the standard.
*Independent practice**	Opportunities given by the teacher for the students to practice the procedure until they attain automaticity.

* Particularly important elements.

- **Step 4. Teach the lesson.** Use the same strategies to teach this lesson as you use for a lesson in any content area.

It is often easier to learn by example. Figure 7.2 describes the process that Katie Fisher, a teacher in Hawaii, follows in order to identify a need of her students, determine an objective, task analyze, plan, and teach a lesson for a procedure. Her process can be modified for any grade or subject area.

Figure 7.2 Process for Teaching Standards, Rules, and Procedures	
Analyze Student Need	On the first day of school, Katie had difficulty getting the students' attention when she needed it. First she tried holding up her hand and blinking the lights. Then she resorted to loudly saying, "Quiet!" Neither strategy worked; too much time was wasted. Katie and her students needed a lesson that established a signal for attention.
Formulate Objective	Katie's objective was to have students respond to the signal "May I have your attention please" by 1. Stopping work. 2. Looking at the teacher. 3. Listening until the teacher says, "Start work." The objective needs to be specific. Katie began with the end in mind.
Analyze Task	Katie broke her objective down into the following component objectives: 1. Learner will know and understand the signal 2. Learner will know and understand teacher behaviors 3. Learner will demonstrate the three behaviors specified in the main objective
Plan Lesson	Katie used the template in Figure 7.1 to plan her lesson on responding to a signal for attention. It is up to the teacher to decide which elements to include.
Teach Lesson	(See main text for Katie's lesson.)

Sample Lesson

Lessons to teach procedures are as different as lessons in any content area. The script, which is included below, contains the exact words that educator Katie Fisher used to teach her students to respond to a signal. This is a directed lesson, and it is a very effective and efficient way to teach students rules and procedures.

But, it is not the *only* way! Katie planned this lesson by using the steps of lesson design (see Figure 7.1).

Anticipatory Set

"Imagine that you are driving along a street and just approaching a corner. You thought there was a stop sign there, but it was not visible. A tree branch was covering it. What might happen?" [Wait time] "If you were thinking, 'I'd be really confused about whether or not to stop,' you'd be exactly right. The stop sign is your signal to stop your car. You don't see it, so you don't know what to do.

"Remember yesterday when I tried to get your attention to give you directions? I flashed the lights, I waved my arm, I finally yelled out, 'Quiet!' It took much too long to get your attention, and you were late to recess. What was the problem?" [Wait time] "Raise your hand if you think it had something to do with confusion over the signal." [Teacher checks hands and asks some students to share their thoughts] "You are right. You did not recognize all my actions as signals. Like the stop sign, it is hard to obey the signal if you don't know what the signal is. And, I had not taught you what the signal would be. We are going to correct that today."

Student Objective

"I thought about this last night, and it seemed to me that the easiest signal to use is for me to say the words, 'May I have your attention, please?' I won't have to run back to the light switch or try to find the bell that I sometimes ring. Today, we're going to learn the signal and the four things you are going to do when I give it."

Purpose

"This procedure will save you a lot of time. You can get the directions or information quickly. Your work will go faster and be easier for you. And you will definitely get to recess on time!"

Input

Teacher lists, explains, and writes the signal she will use and the responses students will make.

- Signal:
    - *"May I have your attention please?"*
- Students will:
    - *Stop working*
        - Teacher: "You will put all supplies on your desk and then fold your hands so you won't be tempted to pick something up or go back to work."

- *Look at the teacher*
  - Teacher: "This lets me know when everyone is ready to listen."
- *Listen*
  - Teacher: "Listening means you empty your head of all the things you are thinking about—work, recess, whatever— and focus on what the speaker is saying. I can't see listening because it goes on inside your head, but you will know if you're doing it."
- *Keep listening until teacher gives the second signal: "Start work."*
  - Teacher: "You won't pick up your pencil and go back to work if I pause for a second or if you think I am through talking. You will keep listening until you hear me give the second signal, 'Start work!'"

Modeling

"Let me show you what it looks like when you respond to the signal." [Student gives the signal, and the teacher models.] "Notice the four important behaviors. I have stopped all work. My pencil is at the top of the desk, and I am folding my hands just to make sure I don't fool around with things on my desk. I am looking right at Shelby [the "teacher" in this scenario], so she knows I am ready. I am listening. I know you can't see that, but I emptied my head of any thoughts about my work, and I am focusing on what Shelby is telling me. I am not going back to work even though Shelby paused for a minute. I am going to wait until she gives the second signal, 'Start work.'"

Check for Understanding

"I want each of you to tell your partner what the signal is for both starting and stopping work." [Wait time; teacher monitors partners' exchanges.] "Now, each of you explain to your partner the four things you do when you hear the signal. I'll walk around to listen. When everyone is finished, I will ask some of you to explain the procedure to the class."

Guided Practice

"It's your turn to practice. Pretend you are writing. I will give you the signal. When you hear it, do the four things you are supposed to do." [Teacher gives signal and monitors performance.] "That's exactly right! Everyone stopped working completely; you are looking at me so I know you are ready; you are listening by focusing just on my words; and everyone is waiting until I say, 'Start work.' Good for you!" [It may be necessary to repeat guided practice several times. Students should practice until they are responding quickly and correctly.]

Closure

"Close your eyes. Picture in your mind my giving you the signal. Think what the words are." [Wait time] "Now imagine yourself doing the four behaviors. Do you have everything out of your hands? Are you looking at me? Did you empty your mind so you can focus on what I will be telling you? Are you continuing to wait until I give the word to begin work? Great! This signal helps us finish our work and stay on schedule."

Independent Practice

Teacher gives signal frequently during the first few days, monitors student performance and gives specific feedback. If performance begins to slip, another practice session is added.

What About High School?

High school teachers often think teaching the procedures in such a detailed way is terribly elementary. Have you ever watched different high school classes enter at the beginning of the period? Why is it that some classes walk in quietly, hand in their homework, sit down to work on the morning sponge activity, and are ready for instruction to begin within five minutes, whereas others are still getting settled 15 minutes after the tardy bell rings? You might have guessed that the first teacher carefully taught beginning-of-class procedures. It is true that the older students have had more socialization in school behavior so they may need less modeling, less practice, and less time spent on procedures. But, no matter how long they have been in school, they have not been socialized in *your* classroom. They don't know how *you* do the sponge activity, they don't know whether *you* want them seated before or after the tardy bell, and they don't know whether *you* want them to leave when the dismissal bell rings or when you excuse them. The only way they will know is if you teach them.

The example of Katie Fisher's directed lesson described above is only one way to teach a standards or procedures lesson. Dave Brees, of Costa Mesa, California, has the students generate suggestions for behaviors that "help them and others to learn" and then come up with their own list. They role-play behaviors that help and hinder, and they finally write an essay in which they commit to a classroom climate that is conducive to learning. A high school computer teacher in Marysville, Washington, Tory Klementsen, spends the first three or four days teaching policies and procedures. She teaches the most important ones and reviews them as necessary. She then assigns the remaining policies to students to teach. They must know and understand the policy, teach it in an interesting way, and review and assess the learning.

The point is that the ideas for teaching standards, rules, and procedures are as varied as the teachers themselves, but effective teachers everywhere, and at all grade levels, teach them. When the teacher takes the time to teach a procedure carefully, it sends a message to students that this is important. Whenever a procedure has been taught, the teacher needs to monitor carefully. As soon as things begin to slip, stop and reteach: "The last time I gave that signal, it took a long time to get everyone's attention. Recall the four behaviors you are supposed to do. Ready? Okay, let's practice."

Posting and Scaffolding

One question that always arises is whether or not standards, rules, and procedures should be posted. If you decide to do so, or if a school rule says you should, then post as few as possible. Perhaps, only the standards should be posted. Certainly every behavior does not need to be officially written down. The more important consideration is do the students *understand* the behavior and can they *do* it with success? As Marilyn Gootman suggests, a good model for teachers is to see themselves as coaches. A coach teaches the game plays explicitly and thoroughly, and provides many opportunities for practice during which time they give suggestions, reminders, and feedback (Gootman, 1997).

Teachers do exactly the same thing. They teach explicitly and then provide help and support as students learn to perform the behaviors automatically and independently. In educational jargon, we refer to these supports as *scaffolds*. Scaffolds are temporary, and they are provided by the teacher. Some supports are modeling, cueing, prompting, guided practice with feedback, and independent practice.

Many times certain procedures are extraordinarily complex. It requires about 19 procedures to prepare high school students for a chemistry lab. The task analysis for working independently has 17 necessary steps. Students can't learn all of these simultaneously, and, yet they must practice all steps every time they go to the lab or work independently. While the chemistry student is learning how to carry the microscope, the teacher is scaffolding for the other 18 steps. When the student can carry the microscope independently, the teacher then demonstrates how to turn it on. Each step is taught separately, and students practice it until they can do it on their own. The chemistry students have to do all 19 steps before they can go to the lab without fear of blowing up the school. The teacher releases the responsibility to the students for what they can do on their own and guides them through the others. Eventually, the 19 steps will be the sole responsibility of the student, but, in the meantime, the teacher supports with scaffolding. The idea of scaffolding is important in classroom management, just as it is in instruction. Students do not come into your classroom with all the skills of self-control and self-management. We don't turn them loose to manage their own behavior until they learn all the steps. We teach them gradually, assist them by scaffolding through the parts they cannot yet do on their own, and then turn each part over to them as they demonstrate their ability to be independent and responsible.

Coaches want their teams to win, just as teachers want their students to be successful. Coaches provide lots of tips throughout the game to their players, and teachers give their students lots of scaffolds throughout instruction. Prompts and cues, such as, "We are going to have a discussion this next hour so it will be important to remember how to respond without raising your hand" or, "When we come in from recess, let's remember to . . ." will help students recall which procedure to follow. Students need to practice the procedure correctly, experience success, and receive supportive and specific feedback on their performance. Scaffolding assists in this process.

Is Teaching the Structure of Management Worth the Time?

Taking time to teach procedures pays off in spades. Once the students know and can do the procedures, your classroom runs smoothly, and you greatly increase learning time. The most frequent classroom management problem that I see is the failure of teachers to explicitly teach the standards, rules, and procedures up front and proactively. They are in a reactive mode from September to June. Every lesson becomes an issue of management, and teaching and learning play second fiddle.

Teaching students self-control and responsibility is an important role for a teacher. These skills are required not only for school but also for living in a democratic society. We must take the time and make the effort to teach our students how to be autonomous, independent, and productive citizens in their community. Much of that is accomplished by teaching students *how* to be autonomous, independent, and productive citizens in their classroom community.

> *　　　　　　　*　　　　　　　*

Once you have taught the structure of the learning environment, and it is firmly in place, you can't just drop the teaching of appropriate behavior and jump into the teaching of content. You don't want all your hard work to be wasted. You want that structure strengthened and maintained. The way to do that is to use strategies of reinforcement, the topic of the next chapter.

8

Reinforcement

The goal of reinforcement is to develop desirable behavior rather than to control misbehavior. The emphasis, where misbehavior occurs, is on pressuring to change, not on exacting retribution.
—Jere Brophy (1988, p. 12)

One thing we dread losing and try to maintain at all costs is our dignity, that feeling of being competent, valued, and in charge of ourselves. When we help our students maintain control of their own behavior, both the teacher and students are working toward the same end. When what we do causes students to lose their dignity, the students and the teacher are juxtaposed, and those students will do whatever they can to fight us (Hunter, 1990).

Establishing and teaching effective standards, rules, and procedures is one important way to help our students maintain control of their behavior. Reinforcement is another. Some of you may visualize drooling dogs, pecking pigeons, or raffle tickets being handed out every time a student breathes correctly. But, Madeline Hunter says, "That is about as far removed from artistic, classroom use of reinforcement theory as opening a can of beans is to culinary art" (1990, p. 3).

We have learned more in the last 25 years about how the brain guides behavior than ever before in history. Much of what we have learned confirms our previous research. Reinforcement theory is still the basis of discipline systems that use any kind of rewards and punishments. Unfortunately, much that you read leaves theory behind and replaces it with a formula. Reinforcement simply does not work that way, and, in thinking that it does, we have lost the power of this principle of learning. So, we are going back to the theory so you can apply it appropriately to *your* class and situation. New research findings suggest ways in which reinforcement can be even more effective than it was previously. Physiological, behavioral, social, and cognitive psychology are now blended to make reinforcement the tool to maintain and strengthen productive behavior and to weaken unproductive behavior. We do that with the objective of teaching students to be in control of themselves. Reinforcement is neither manipulative nor controlling. Rather, it teaches students to be good problem solvers, to make sound decisions, and to be in charge of their own behavior. The appropriate application of the principles of reinforcement by teachers makes the difference between chaotic classrooms and those in which students are responsibly in charge of themselves.

Reinforcement is difficult. First, it is objective, not emotional. It is not easy to be objective when a student has just interrupted your beautifully designed lesson for the 15th time! Second, reinforcement requires teachers to put themselves in the students' shoes. We have to determine what will be a reinforcer for the *student*. What will the student like or dislike? What is a reinforcer for one student may not be for another. Finally, reinforcement theory is often misunderstood. There have been too many translations; it is often presented as a prescription for teachers to apply without considering the student or the situation. Although it is the foundation of virtually all discipline systems, it often is not done appropriately. The goal of this chapter is to present the principles of reinforcement, so you will understand them well enough to be able to adjust for the needs of your students.

In education, when we discuss reinforcement, we are talking about ways to strengthen productive behavior and to weaken unproductive behavior. We use both to teach new behaviors and to maintain those already in place. Reinforcement is based on the idea that there are factors in the environment that determine whether a behavior will occur. People do things that pay off, and they avoid things that don't. In every classroom, we have behaviors that we would like to strengthen and those we would like to weaken. When Jere Brophy (1994, P. 44) defines management as "structuring the environment so students can learn," reinforcement is one way we do it. We don't leave reinforcement to random and unpredictable environmental factors. *We* structure the environment so that productive behaviors pay off and unproductive ones do not. There are three principles of reinforcement— positive, negative, and extinction. We are going to consider each of these in terms of four issues (Wiseman, 1995):

1. What it is
2. What it does
3. Things to know about it
4. Types of reinforcers

Positive Reinforcement

What It Is

Positive reinforcement is the process of following a behavior with something wanted or needed by the students. Figure 8.1 gives a visual representation of positive reinforcement.

Figure 8.1
Positive Reinforcement

$$PR = B \longrightarrow DS$$

PR = Positive reinforcement
B = Behavior
DS = Desired stimulus

What It Does

Positive reinforcement strengthens the original behavior.

Example: I go to a new hairstylist. Friends say, "Your hair looks fabulous!" I go to the same hairstylist the next time I get my hair cut. A compliment is a desired stimulus for me.

Example: Student turns in work on time. I write a complimentary note. Student turns in work on time tomorrow. A note is a desired stimulus for the student.

Things to Know

Meaningful

A desired stimulus must be meaningful, that is, something that the student wants or needs.

Example: A compliment is only a desired stimulus for one who likes compliments. If I had been the type of person who is embarrassed by public attention and compliments, I may have not returned to the hairstylist responsible for my garnering those comments.

Example: A positive note is only a desired stimulus for one who likes positive notes. Some students do not like the attention focused on them that praise brings. When this is the case, they avoid doing whatever it is that prompts it.

Specific

Be specific in labeling the behaviors that you want strengthened. If you are too general in your feedback, students do not know which part of what they are doing you want strengthened.

Example: "Stanley, you are here right on time this morning, 8:15 a.m." If the teacher had recognized the behavior with a general comment such as "Good job," Stanley would not know whether his teacher was referring to his hairstyle, his promptness, or his swagger. The chances that Stanley, or any student, will intuitively know which specific behavior the teacher wants strengthened without the teacher labeling it are slim to none. If it is the on-time behavior that you want strengthened, rather than the swaggering or the arranging of his hair, then you will want to give specific feedback on promptness.

Immediate

The closer to the time the behavior occurred the reinforcer is, the more effective it will be.

Example: "You came in quietly this morning, put things away quickly in the closet, and got right to work on your sponge activity." These positive words are said the minute the students accomplish the behavior. To wait until time to go home to reinforce morning behavior is to lose the effect of the reinforcer. By afternoon the student has no recollection of how he or she came in that morning. The student cannot possibly repeat the behavior with any degree of accuracy.

Types of Positive Reinforcers

There are three main categories of positive reinforcers, and they are hierarchical—the social reinforcers are the only ones that will teach self-control. Figure 8.2 shows the categories arranged in order from the one that has the greatest effect on the development of student self-discipline to the one that has the least. Start at the top and, if it is not effective, then move down until you reach one that is. The key is, wherever you begin on the hierarchy, try to move closer to the social reinforcers at the top. They are powerful influences in the development of students who are autonomous, responsible, and in charge of their own behavior.

Figure 8.2
Hierarchy of Positive Reinforcers

Key idea: Start at the top of the hierarchy, moving down only if the first reinforcers you try are ineffective. If you find it necessary to begin at a lower place on the hierarchy, pair the reinforcer you use with positive feedback. When you can, remove the lower-level reinforcer, retaining only the feedback. This will help you move back toward self-control at the top of the hierarchy.

Social Reinforcer
Specific, positive feedback from a "significant other." Most effective at developing student self-control.

Privilege Reinforcer
Something the student values that is not routinely accorded to everyone (e.g., free time or no homework).

Tangible Reinforcer
Something that can be seen or touched.

- *Best:* Student receives a symbol of the positive behavior (e.g., a certificate or stickers).
- *Next best:* Student maintains a private record of the positive behavior.
- *Last resort:* Student receives a prize that is not connected to the behavior that earned it (e.g., a raffle ticket or candy).

Least effective at developing student self-control.

Note: Adapted from *Discipline That Develops Self-Discipline* (Hunter, 1990).

Social Reinforcers

Social reinforcers are those that are socially mediated by a teacher or parent. In this case, we are talking specifically about positive messages given to a student by a *significant other*—and a teacher *is* a significant other. The significant other is not to be overlooked. The impact of a social reinforcer is directly affected by the relationship between the *giver*, the teacher, and the *receiver*, the student. We discussed in Chapter 5 that the teacher who is perceived by the student as caring and trusting has more influence than one who is not. The importance of a warm and friendly relationship with a student whose behavior you are trying to strengthen, or change, cannot be underestimated. Positive messages from someone the student detests are not likely to have much effect! The stronger the relationship a teacher has with a child, the more effective a positive message will be.

Social reinforcers, positive messages from a significant other, are the top of the hierarchy, not because they are best and not because they are right, but because they are the only ones that help students reach the goal of self-discipline. In order to make them the most powerful in terms of a reinforcer, these positive messages require two attributes:

Emphasizing effort as the cause of success, rather than ability, luck, or the ease of the task. The reason for this is that effort is under the student's control, and it is the only one of the four possible attributions to success that *is*. To tell the student he was successful because he put forth effort or that he was not successful because of lack of effort is to attribute the cause to something the student can control. It develops an internal locus. It puts the student in charge.

Using "you" messages rather than "I" messages. "You" messages put the responsibility on the students. They can also accept the credit for a job well done. To say, "You worked hard this week on those math problems. You must feel very proud of that fine grade you received on your test," is to let the student know it is his or her accomplishment, that he or she is the one who is responsible for the grade because he or she put forth the effort. The credit is all his or hers. When we give "I" messages such as, "I am so proud of you for getting that A," we are making this accomplishment all about *us* and how we feel. How we feel is not relevant. We don't want our students getting good grades to please us. We want them getting good grades to please themselves. We label these accomplishments for students, so they know what an accomplishment is and what feelings go along with it. These feelings are for them to experience and enjoy, which they can now do because we helped them realize that success resulted from *their* effort and is under *their* control. This is the real way to empower your students. When they know that success or failure is under their own control, they begin to take responsibility for their behavior.

Examples of positive messages that attribute a student's effort through "you" messages include the following:

- "You worked hard. Now you have some free time to read a book of your choice."
- "You certainly are able to get started quickly."
- "You must feel proud of your success in the track meet. Your practice paid off for you."
- "You must have been thinking deeply to have that kind of insight."
- "You're always on time, so we can get started quickly."
- "You listened carefully to be able to do that so well."
- "Your hard work really paid off. Excellent!"
- "You have a real knack for adding personal examples to your writing."
- "You did some excellent thinking to discover that attribute."

- "Your careful work resulted in a perfect paper."
- "You are working so hard at determining importance as you read. You must notice the difference it is making in your comprehension."

Notice there is not an "I" message in the bunch. Not, "I like the way you got started so quickly," or "I am so proud of you today." "I" messages are the teacher controlling the student. The student's behavior is valued because the teacher likes it, not because the student made a good decision about it. This can be seen as manipulative because the student is trying to figure out what the teacher wants him to do rather than what he or she thinks is the right thing to do. We want our students to self-monitor and self-assess. Successful people give themselves feedback all day long. Our feedback is a model for the kind that students will eventually give themselves. We give feedback to students as a scaffold until they can assume the responsibility for this assessment on their own. "You" messages promote an internal locus of control for the student.

Privilege Reinforcers

A privilege is the next in the hierarchy. It can be very effective, and, if the positive message does not work initially, then move down to the privilege. A privilege is something valued by the *student* that is not routinely accorded to everyone. To be most effective, it should be related to the behavior that earned it. When a privilege is awarded, it should be paired with a positive comment. Eventually, the privilege can be withdrawn, and just the comment continued as a reinforcer. This way, you are helping the student develop self-control.

Examples of privilege reinforcers include:

- "You worked hard today. You can spend some free time reading in the library."
- "You finished quickly. Perhaps you can assist someone in your group."
- "You have really mastered the concept of long division. You will not need to do any more problems."
- "You worked hard to finish your reading. You won't have any homework this evening."

Tangible Reinforcers

These are the kinds of reinforcer that can be touched, seen, or hung on the refrigerator. They are the least effective because they are furthest down the hierarchy from the reinforcer that develops self-control. This doesn't mean you can't use them. It does mean that you shouldn't start here, but only move here if the feedback or privileges are not effective. It also means if you are at this level, continue trying to move the student up the hierarchy toward feedback alone. Within this category of tangible reinforcers, there are several kinds:

- **Best of the tangibles:** Symbol of the behavior that earned it. This includes certificates, notes, and stickers.
- **Next best:** Student keeps a *private* record of each occurrence of productive behavior. To make such records public can be embarrassing.
- **The last resort:** These are the least effective for developing self-control because they are not connected to the behavior that earned them. The student may be performing the behavior for the reward rather than for any internal feeling of satisfaction. These kinds of rewards, such as raffle tickets, candy, and toys, reduce intrinsic motivation and should be avoided if possible.

Positive reinforcement is almost always effective and does not bring with it any of the concerns that we find with the other two principles—negative reinforcement and extinction.

Negative Reinforcement

What It Is
Negative reinforcement is the process of following a behavior with something not wanted or needed by the student (an aversive stimulus). Any action that removes the aversive stimulus is reinforced. Negative reinforcement results in a person avoiding an aversive stimulus by replacing the original behavior with a new one. See Figure 8.3 for a visual of negative reinforcement.

What It Does
Negative reinforcement strengthens the *replacement* behavior (B_2)—whatever behavior gets rid of the aversive stimulus. We have all had the experience of exceeding the speed limit, viewing the police car in our rearview mirror, and slowing down, thus avoiding a ticket. Good driving behavior is negatively reinforced. The replacement behavior (slowing down) is strengthened.

Negative reinforcement is not punishment because it leaves the person in control. I had my choice to slow down to avoid a ticket. With punishment, there is no choice. The punishment is given, and the person cannot avoid it. It is true, however, that a punishment given one day can become the negative reinforcer the next. I had to get a ticket before I decided it was worth it to slow down when the police car loomed in my rearview mirror.

Figure 8.3
Negative Reinforcement

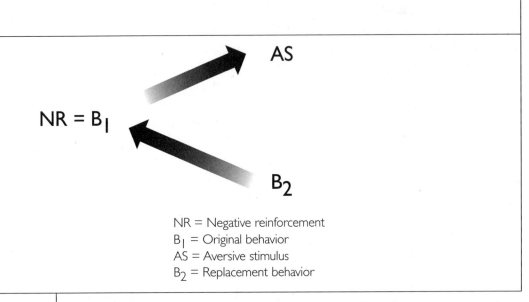

NR = Negative reinforcement
B_1 = Original behavior
AS = Aversive stimulus
B_2 = Replacement behavior

Think of positive reinforcement as *adding* (+) something the person wants or needs. Think of negative reinforcement as *subtracting* (–) a penalty the person does *not* want or need. Both positive and negative reinforcements strengthen a behavior. Positive strengthens the *original* behavior. Negative strengthens a *replacement* behavior (Welsh, 1987).

Example: "I wear a seatbelt when I drive because I like the feeling of safety and security that it gives me. That feeling is a *desired stimulus* for me. It adds a feeling of comfort that strengthens my seatbelt behavior. Good seatbelt behavior, my original behavior, is *positively* reinforced for me because something pleasant is added.

"My daughter wears a seatbelt because she wants to avoid (subtract) the buzzer that goes off unrelentingly when the seatbelt is not fastened. The buzzer is an *aversive stimulus* for her. It is annoying, and the only way she avoids it is to fasten her seatbelt. Good seatbelt behavior, the replacement behavior, is *negatively* reinforced for her. She avoids something unpleasant by changing her original behavior to a new one. Note the result of both positive and negative reinforcement is the same—appropriate seatbelt behavior is strengthened. You can combine positive and negative reinforcement to change a behavior, or you can use one or the other. You may not know which one is working, and it really doesn't matter. The important thing is that the correct behavior is in place."

Things To Know

Meaningful

The aversive stimulus needs to be meaningful to the student, who must dislike it more than he or she likes doing what it is you want stopped. Sending a student to the office only works if the student hates the office. Missing recess only works if the student hates missing recess. For the students who enjoy the excitement of the office, or who enjoy staying in the room because they don't know how to socialize on the playground, these aversive stimuli are actually desired stimuli. Poor behavior is positively reinforced! This is the reason that a set list, or hierarchy, of consequences does not work. What is a consequence for one student is a reward for another. An aversive stimulus is defined by its result. It is only effective if it is aversive to a specific person in a specific situation.

Specific

Specificity has a whole different meaning when it comes to negative reinforcement. A major drawback of negative reinforcement is the unpredictability of the replacement behavior. Selecting the new behavior to replace the old one cannot be left for the student to choose. The teacher must be very specific in determining exactly what the new behavior will be and articulating it to the student. If not, the new behavior may be far worse than the old. If Billy is tapping his desk with his pencil and the teacher glares, Billy knows what *not to do*. The problem is that he does not know what *to do*. He may well begin to tap Claudia unless the teacher clearly states the alternative behavior. "Billy, tapping your desk with the pencil is disruptive to the class. Please put it inside your desk" identifies a specific replacement behavior. It also saves Claudia's head and, at the same time, saves you from getting into a power struggle with Billy. Negative reinforcement used without a specific replacement behavior identified by the teacher can be dangerous. Lying and cheating, for example, are most often the result of improper use of negative reinforcement.

Example: A student fails to do his homework and is given detention (aversive stimulus), which he hates. The next night the student replaces not doing homework with copying his friend's homework. The teacher had no way of knowing this happened, so says, "Good for you, Dave. You will not have detention today." Cheating, the replacement behavior selected by Dave, has now been positively reinforced. Dave's new behavior is cheating rather than completing homework.

Types of Negative Reinforcers

The negative reinforcers included here have three criteria in common (Hunter, 1990) They

- Preserve the dignity of the student.

- Encourage the development of self-discipline.
- Have a high probability of being successful.

Negative reinforcement puts the students in charge. Unlike punishment, an aversive stimulus in negative reinforcement can be avoided when the student changes his or her behavior. The aversive stimulus is withdrawn as soon as the student changes from inappropriate to appropriate behavior. Remember that the purpose of negative reinforcement is to change behavior, not punish it.

Aversive stimuli are both nonverbal and verbal (Savage, 1999). Nonverbal are the least disruptive and should be the first types used.

Nonverbal Responses

Facial expressions. The well-known *teacher look* fits into this category. It can be extremely effective. If you are a new teacher, practice the *look* carefully (use a mirror to monitor) until it is perfect. It will serve you well throughout your career!

Eye contact. Brief eye contact with the offending student can be just what it takes to move him or her back on task. Remember, as soon as the misbehavior is corrected, the contact (aversive stimulus) is withdrawn.

Gestures. Holding up your hand as a signal to stop, shaking or nodding your head, and leaning in toward the students are examples of gestures that can be effective.

Proximity. One of the most useful strategies is to increase your proximity to a misbehaving student. Delivering instruction near a student who engages in inappropriate behavior prevents much of it from happening. Or, standing next to a student who is currently off task is an effective way to get him back on task. This is called MBWA, or management by walking around. It not only works to prevent misbehavior in the first place, but it also corrects it once it begins.

Removing distractions. Especially with young children, simply walking up and removing the toy or whatever gadget is attracting the student's attention is an effective management technique. When the student is back on task, the confiscated item is returned, so the student can retain control of the situation. He knows he can avoid permanent loss of his or her treasure by correcting misbehavior.

Waiting. A frequently used strategy by the most effective class managers is simply to stop talking, stand quietly, and wait. The secret here is to wait until all students are doing what they are supposed to be doing. If you try to rush this and resume instruction before everyone is ready, you reinforce the idea that it is okay to not pay attention.

Recording student behavior. Nothing is quite as effective as walking quietly over to the student with a clipboard, standing close beside the desk, and recording exactly what is being said or done. No one likes to have their behavior documented. Students don't know what you plan to do with this record, who will see it, or what its purpose is. Students want to avoid this uncertainty, an aversive stimulus, by quickly resuming appropriate behavior. And, when they do, you quit writing and move away. It is important that students make the connection between their behavior and the aversive stimulus. They need to know they can get rid of the stimulus by choosing the correct behavior. What results from students' behavior is their responsibility and under their control.

Verbal Responses

Using student's name in a positive way. For a student who is temporarily off task, hearing his own name used by you in the context of your instruction acts as an alerting reflex to get him back on task. Saying "If we were reading a story about Al . . . " gets Al's attention and gets him back with you. Or, "Shelby, will you act as recorder for us during this next activity?" keeps Shelby attentive and lets her know that you know she has not been! This is never done in a way that embarrasses a student or puts him or her on the spot. You would not say, "Jake, give us the answer to the question I just asked," if you know Jake has not been listening. But, you might say, "Jake, I'll be asking you to share your ideas on the next question." This gets Jake back on track and retains his dignity at the same time. Remember your goal is not to punish but to get Al, Shelby, and Jake back on task.

Reminders, prompts, and cues. These are given privately to individual students by quietly walking over to them, stating the reminder, and moving away. This is not the time for a discussion, only a prompt about what the student should be doing. These prompts and cues can also be used for the whole class. There are four ways to phrase them—as

1. Descriptive statements,
2. Enforceable statements,
3. Questions, and
4. Choices.

All four are descriptive, not prescriptive. The teacher simply describes the situation or frames a choice, and the decision as to what to do about it is left to the students. This keeps them in control and allows them to develop self-discipline, problem-solving, and good decision-making. Appropriate choices and decisions not only teach self-control, but allow the student to avoid an aversive stimulus.

Descriptive statements describe the situation but leave it to the student to determine the action to be taken:

- "It's almost time for a break."
- "Papers will be due in seven minutes."
- "It is nearly time to change classes."

Enforceable statements (Fay & Funk, 1995) tell the students what the teacher will do and under what conditions he or she will do it. They do not tell the student what to do. The student's response is under his or her control. Notice the statements are phrased positively to be an authentic choice; when phrased negatively, they become threats, not choices:

- "I listen to people who raise their hand." (Not, "I will not listen to you until you raise your hand.")
- "When everything is cleaned up, I will excuse you for lunch."
- "When everyone is quiet, I will begin reading."

Questions alert students more directly about inappropriate behavior:

- "Jean, are you aware that your pencil tapping is disturbing your group?"
- "Julie, would you read silently? Your voice is distracting the people sitting near you."
- "Brad, do you realize your humming is distracting to others in the class?"

Choices (Fay & Funk, 1995) keep the students in control and avoid power struggles. No one wants to be continually told what to do. People must feel some control over their own lives. If we share as much control with our students as we can, they are willing to give us the reins when we need them. Giving students authentic choices, whenever it is possible, is a way of sharing control. It is also a way to teach decision making and responsibility. The choice that is given should be acceptable to both teacher and student. This is *not* a choice between the behavior the teacher wants and a punishment. We are talking about legitimate choices for students to make. There are a hundred ways each day that a teacher offers choices to students:

- "Would you rather work alone or with your group?"
- "Feel free to do the first 10 problems or the last 10."
- "Which do you prefer, sitting in rows or in a circle?"

Negative reinforcement is as powerful as positive reinforcement in terms of strengthening productive behavior and weakening unproductive behavior. It is important to remember that it is not without the side effect of a poor replacement behavior being selected. There are no concerns about the use of positive reinforcement. You can't go wrong there. But, with negative reinforcement, care must be given to the selection of the new behavior.

Extinction

The third strategy of reinforcement is extinction. This is actually the strategy of using no reinforcement at all.

What It Is
Extinction is a behavior followed by no reinforcement, as seen in Figure 8.4.

Figure 8.4
Extinction

$$E = B \longrightarrow 0$$

E = Extinction
B = Behavior
0 = No reinforcement

What It Does
Extinction stops or diminishes behavior.

Things to Know
There are four important questions to ask yourself when you make the decision whether to use the extinction strategy:

Question 1: Is it a new behavior? If the behavior is relatively new, extinction usually stops it quickly. If this is the first time a student has said a four-letter word, ignoring it will probably extinguish the behavior right away.

Question 2: Is it an old behavior or a habit? A long-standing behavior (habit) gets worse before it gets better. The question that you must ask yourself is, "How much escalation can I stand?" If the student has been saying four-letter words since kindergarten and he is now a 6th grader, he will undoubtedly say more four-letter words, say them louder, and say them more frequently before the behavior diminishes. You may not want this escalation, in which case extinction is not the strategy to use.

Question 3: Who is the student's audience? If a student is behaving in a particular way to get your attention, and you ignore him or her, extinction will be effective. If peers are the audience and they are reinforcing the misbehavior, it will be strengthened. Often you can get peers to stop reinforcement—to stop laughing at the culprit's jokes, for example—but, if you can't, don't use extinction.

Question 4: What is the intentionality? We often use extinction unintentionally on our students' good behavior by forgetting to positively reinforce it. When we do, it is extinguished! It is very important to remember to continue to reinforce good behavior when you see it, or it quickly goes away. Reinforcement strategies can be spaced farther and farther apart, but remembering to give positive feedback every few weeks on behavior that is in place pays huge dividends for you.

*   *   *

Reinforcement theory is powerful. It teaches and strengthens appropriate behavior, and it also maintains it over time. Teaching prosocial behavior is part of what we do, and reinforcement theory is invaluable in this process. Are there times when consequences must be administered and when teaching through instruction and strategies of reinforcement are not effective? Yes, although they are not as frequent as you might think. When you have a student who has not responded to the instruction and reinforcement of appropriate behavior, it is time to move into your backup plan.

9

The Backup System

*When discipline problems occur, the challenge to the teacher is
how to intervene in a manner which encourages continued positive
growth and, at the same time, restores appropriate student behavior. To the extent that these interventions are preplanned and systematic, rather than shooting from the hip and arbitrary, the
probability of their effectiveness is increased.*
    —James Levin and John Shanken-Kaye (1996, p. 105)

The first rule to learn about the backup system is to do everything you possibly
can to avoid using it! The backup system is *intervention.* Effective management is
based on *prevention.* The key ideas in this book are mostly about prevention: managing time and space; teaching and reinforcing classroom standards, rules, and
procedures; and structuring instructional strategies so misbehavior does not occur.
These strategies will prevent 90 percent of your management problems. But what
about the 10 percent that are not preventable and that have not changed through
use of reinforcement strategies? They require the backup system.

What Is the Backup System?

The backup system kicks in when prevention has not been successful. Disciplinary
interventions must be taken to elicit changes in the behavior of students who fail
to meet expectations, especially misbehavior that is salient or sustained enough to
disrupt the classroom management system. The backup system is designed to suppress disruptions and pressure students to correct misbehavior. You will notice in
Figure 9.1 that it is integrated with the reinforcement system discussed in the previous chapter. Together they form a hierarchy of both prevention and intervention

strategies that makes up the system for teaching appropriate behavior before the fact, and changing misbehavior after the fact.

Figure 9.1
Hierarchy of Management Strategies

Prevention

Positive reinforcement
- Social reinforcers
- Privilege reinforcers
- Tangible reinforcers

Negative reinforcement

Nonverbal
- Facial expressions
- Eye contact
- Gestures
- Proximity
- Removal of distractions
- Waiting
- Recording of student behavior

Verbal
- Positive use of student's name
- Reminders, prompts, and cues (e.g., descriptive statements, enforceable statements, questions, and choices)

Extinction

Intervention

Demand

Consequence
- Restitution
- Restoration
- Restriction
- Reflection

Individual intervention plan

Outside referrals (from school administrators, support personnel, or outside professionals)

Note: Adapted from *The Self-Control Classroom* (Levin & Shanken-Kaye, 1996).

The backup system cannot function on its own, and it is structured with the same care as the rest of the system. In the previous chapter, we discussed the strengthening of productive behavior and the weakening of unproductive behavior through reinforcement theory. Appropriate behavior is strengthened by positive reinforcement, and very low-key disruptions are handled through the use of negative reinforcement and extinction. These strategies focus on the teaching of self-control, responsibility, and the prevention or nonescalation of misbehavior. They are the foundation for the intervention strategies, which, for the first time, introduce negative sanctions into the hierarchy. Without the teaching of responsibility and limits through reinforcement, intervention will be overused. And overuse means abuse. We back ourselves into a corner if we jump to intervention before the foundation is laid through all the strategies of prevention we have discussed in this book. Negative sanctions, used too early, destroy the relationship between teachers and students. Intervention strategies must be used with great care, and only after a trusting relationship is built and a firm foundation is in place.

Even when we enter intervention with all the pieces in place, we are going down a difficult path. Moving from prevention to intervention is a more serious step than you might think. It requires careful planning. Winging it at this point is definitely not recommended! We need to know exactly what we are doing. If a crisis occurs, we can be put into a very serious situation. Intervention is confrontational, so it carries more concern. Negative sanctions are not to be taken lightly, even though the strategies are still focused on changing (not punishing) behavior and developing student self-control rather than expecting mere compliance.

Guidelines for Intervention

Levin and Shanken-Kaye (1996) discuss the necessity for intervention guidelines. The guidelines help ensure that we do not increase a student's sense of failure, and that an internal locus of control is maintained. This is not about teacher control; it is about pressuring to change. The guidelines are:

- Provide the student with maximum opportunity for controlling his or her behavior appropriately.
- Make sure the intervention is not more disruptive to the class than the student's behavior.
- Minimize the possibility of confrontation.
- Protect the physical and psychological safety of the student, the class, and the teacher.

- Leave open the greatest number of opportunities for further intervention. A first intervention may not work, and it is important that teachers have additional options. The hierarchy, presented in this chapter, provides them.

Intervention Strategies

Demands

The first intervention strategy, when all prevention strategies have failed, is to make a demand on the student. This needs to be carefully planned and implemented so confrontation is not excessive. A demand is more effective if you tell the student exactly what *to do*, rather than what *not to do*:

- "David, get your book out and begin your reading." (Not, "Stop wandering around the room.")
- "Bonnie, put your sweater in the closet and start your sponge activity."
- "You have three problems to finish. Get started."
- "Barbara, sit at your desk."

The way you state a demand is as important as the words you use. State it privately and quietly to students. Be firm, but not harsh. This preserves their dignity and yours! It also lessens the possibility of a power struggle, which often emerges because a publicly reprimanded student must preserve his ego in front of peers. This need is considerably less if the audience is removed. Here are a few suggestions to keep in mind when making demands of your students:

- Speak seriously and assertively, but not angrily or aggressively.
- Maintain constant eye contact.
- Use as few words as possible. This is not the time to bring up past misdeeds or comment about the future. Your objective here is to stop inappropriate behavior now. Don't get off track. Don't threaten. Don't use statements such as "This is the third time I've told you . . ." or "Will you ever learn?" These are not effective and destroy the directness of the demand.
- Fred Jones (1987, p. 98) describes the process of "moving in" and "moving out." You may want to move in very close to the student. If the student is at his desk, kneel down so you are at eye level, lean in,

and talk quietly and seriously. Make your demand. Remain in place. If the student has trouble with his work, you do not help him at this time. Your objective, remember, is to stop misbehavior, not offer assistance. Stay in place observing the student until he is doing what he is supposed to be doing. Wait a few seconds longer. Say, "Thank you," and walk away. Again, you want the student to see the connection between your demand and his behavior. When his behavior is corrected, you move away. If the behavior stays appropriate, you don't mention it again.

Consequences

All of us, including students, need to assume responsibility and make amends for our inappropriate behavior. That is where consequences come in. Consequences are different from punishment (Gootman, 1997) in that they:

Flow logically from what the student did. They are related to the misbehavior, and they make sense. There is a cause-effect relationship between behavior and consequences. Punishments are not connected to what the student did wrong. Consequences teach appropriate behavior; punishments only suppress misbehavior.

- **Example:** A student takes his friend's favorite pencil.
- **Consequence:** The student brings a new pencil for his friend to replace the one he took.
- **Punishment:** The student misses recess for the day.

Hold the child accountable for his or her behavior. The responsibility for correction is the student's. The student is required to correct the damage or harm caused by the misbehavior whenever possible. Punishments place the responsibility for correction in the hands of the teacher.

- **Example:** One student hits another.
- **Consequence:** Student is required to think of a way to make up the hurt to the other student and to come up with options for handling disagreements more appropriately in the future.
- **Punishment:** Student is required to miss the assembly on Friday.

Keep the child's dignity intact. Punishments are often humiliating.

- **Example:** A student lies to the teacher about homework.
- **Consequence:** Student completes work during recess.

- **Punishment:** The teacher accuses the child of being a liar in front of the class.

It is the consensus of most researchers that punishment is not effective in reducing inappropriate behavior or increasing the likelihood of increasing appropriate behavior (Levin & Shanken-Kaye, 1996). If it were, discipline problems would not be an issue, because punishment is the dominant feature of most teachers' repertoires of discipline strategies. Punishment does not teach alternate acceptable behaviors; in fact, it models just the opposite. Teachers use punishment out of anger, frustration, or lack of other strategies. Consequences, however, teach students the connection between how they choose to behave and the outcomes of that behavior. Consequences are teaching tools to be used when misbehavior cannot be prevented or stopped by strategies higher on the hierarchy.

Marilyn Gootman identifies four categories of consequences (1997):

- Restitution
- Restoration
- Restriction
- Reflection

Restitution. When someone destroys or loses someone else's property, the responsible thing to do is fix or replace it. If a student tears a classmate's book, then the responsible consequence is for him to replace it or pay for it. If a student writes on the desk, he needs to clean it off. When a student has wasted the teacher's time, he needs to pay it back by staying in and helping her with a task. When a student is ill or late, he is responsible for finding out what work is missed. How a student makes restitution may be a decision for him to make. You can assist and support the student in this process.

Restoration. When students get out of control they often need time away from the class to restore and collect themselves so they function well with others. A student might be moved to the time-out corner. An older student can take a seat at the back of the classroom. Or, perhaps, you have an arrangement with another teacher to send a student to her class for a temporary respite. The point is that the misbehaving student is given some time and space to pull himself or herself together.

Restriction. Temporarily restricting privileges that students have abused is a logical consequence for the student who is careless with a computer, who doesn't clean up centers, who is disruptive during an assembly, or who has difficulty with the softball rules during a class game. She simply is restricted for a given length of time from using the computer, going to centers or to an assembly, or playing soft-ball with her class. Sometimes the student can use the time to observe other students' appropriate behavior. This gives the student some concrete ideas about her or his own action plan.

Reflection. One of the most effective consequences for misbehavior is to have a student reflect on what has happened and devise a plan so the misbehavior does not reoccur. Problem solving is an important tool for students. Often the student misbehaved because he did not have more acceptable options. Reflection can provide those for the student. The teacher can make suggestions about how others have handled the situation, but the solution results from the student's own reflection.

Student Choice of Consequences

Is there ever a time when the students should have a choice of consequences? Absolutely. Much will depend on the degree of misbehavior, but giving choices, where possible, helps students to retain some control. Fay and Funk (1995) emphasize the value of giving students a choice of consequences (e.g., "I can meet with you at 12:15 or 3:15. Which do you prefer?" "Would you rather complete your homework at recess or lunch?").

Notice that by the time you are at this level of the hierarchy, the choice is not about having or not having a consequence. That choice was possible in the prevention stage, but not here. Still, there is no reason if it is possible, that the student should not have some voice in the consequence. This often avoids a power struggle and preserves the relationship between teacher and student.

Whatever the consequences of their choices, they need to be allowed to play out. Your response to an undesirable outcome should be given with empathy—"How sad. I know you wanted to play soccer during recess instead of finishing that assignment." When students make choices and the consequences fall, they can only blame themselves.

Posting Consequences

Teachers often wonder whether consequences should be posted along with the standards. My suggestion is that they should not be. First of all, there is no set list of consequences. What is a consequence for one is a reward for another. Consequences must be meaningful to the students receiving them. Second, when standards are established and posted, there is an expectation from both teacher and students that they will be met. With the list of consequences on the same chart, the message is pretty loud and clear: "Here are the standards. We don't expect you to live up to them, so this is what happens when you fail." I don't recommend posting anything but standards. If a discipline plan needs to go home, we suggest something like the plan in Figure 9.2 for elementary students.

Figure 9.2
Sample Elementary School Behavior Plan

Standard
Be polite and helpful

Rewards
Learning as much as we can
Belonging to a caring and cooperative classroom

Consequences
If needed, handled privately between the student and teacher

Figure 9.3 offers a possible example for secondary students.

Figure 9.3
Sample Secondary School Behavior Plan

Standard
Do only those things that allow you and others to learn

Rewards
Be an expert in economics, chemistry, literature, etc.
Participate in a learning community

Consequences
If needed, handled privately between the student and teacher

You will want to think and plan carefully about the consequences you use at this point. The effort you put into making them effective will be worth it. If the student is not successful here, you have to move down on the hierarchy. The next steps require much more of your time and energy.

Individual Intervention Plan

You may have one or two students who simply are not responding to any of the strategies you have tried—either to prevent misbehavior or to intervene with demands or consequences when it has already occurred. These students need individual, systematic, and focused assistance and support as they work to change their behavior. It is time for the individual plan, designed specifically for the needs of the particular student. The principles are still the same—you want the student to develop responsibility and self-control. But, the pressure to do so may need to be more focused and intensified.

Principles of an Intervention Plan

In his article, "Educating Teachers About Managing Classrooms and Students," Jere Brophy outlines the following principles of an intervention plan (1988):

- Minimize power struggles by talking with the student in private.
- Be sure the student is aware of the behavior and understands why it is not appropriate.
- Be sure the systematic intervention hierarchy has been followed.
- Get the student to accept responsibility and commit to change.
- Provide any needed modeling or instruction.
- Work with the student to develop a mutually agreeable plan to solve the problem.
- Concentrate on developing desirable behavior rather than controlling misbehavior.
- Project positive expectations, attributions, and social labels.
- If consequences are necessary, the emphasis should be on pressuring to change, not exacting retribution.

Sample Intervention Plan

An individual plan is just that—individual. There is no *formula*, but Figure 9.4 shows what a plan looks like. You will see the principles identified above embedded within it. This sample plan is for a student who has been repeatedly calling out instead of raising his or her hand, but the elements of the plan can be generalized to many behaviors.

Figure 9.4
Sample Intervention Plan

For one day, tally the number of times the problem occurs (e.g., calling out). Data matters! Following this, meet privately with the student to discuss the problem. During the meeting, be sure to attend to the following:

- Explain the problem behavior.
- Present evidence of frequency.
- Explain the reasons that behavior cannot continue. This is *not* a discussion; this is a rationale. Be firm, but calm. Ask the student these questions: "What should you do when you want to enter the discussion?" and, "Would it help to know what other kids did who had this problem?" (This lets student know others have been in this situation and were able to handle it.)
- Have the student select the option she is going to try. Make sure she understands the behavior: can she explain what she *should* be doing? Can she perform the behavior correctly? If necessary, teach the appropriate behavior and have the student practice. Role-playing can help. Make sure the student is confident that she can carry out the new behavior successfully.
- Assure the student that you know she can change her behavior and that you are willing to do whatever she needs to support her efforts. It is *her* problem, and she will need to change, but you are on her side to make sure she is successful.
- Have the student commit in writing to change her behavior. Hold her absolutely accountable to abide by terms of signed document.
- Set goals for the first day. How much less often will inappropriate behavior occur? You may need to count reductions in inappropriate behavior, but if possible, focus on the positive by counting how many times the student performs the new, appropriate behavior. Make goals very realistic: "You called out 25 times today. Do you think you could reduce that to 20 tomorrow?"

Following the meeting, have the student keep a private record of violations or examples of positive behaviors. You can help by reminding the student when to tally, but your reminder should not be punitive. The student and teacher should work together to correct behavior. You are not trying to catch the student behaving inappropriately. Prompt or cue the student many times at first to set her up for success, such as:

- "What are you going to remember to do today? What is your goal?"
- "This next hour might be a difficult time. What are you going to focus on? Can I help you?"
- "I'm going to be asking questions about the story we read. I know you will have some great responses. What will you need to remember?"

Respond positively and privately to student's efforts:

- "You remembered to raise your hand. Good for you."
- Put a comment on a sticky note and put on the student's desk. They enjoy these. Sticky notes are also good ways to prompt the student or remind her of her goal (e.g., "The next 15 minutes will be discussion. What will you need to remember?").

Figure 9.4
Sample Intervention Plan (continued)

After school, review the day's record with the student:

- Discuss how much the misbehavior was reduced. Have the student analyze strategies she used to remember appropriate behavior.
- It might be helpful to suggest that the student watch a neighbor. When the neighbor raises his hand, the student will be reminded to do the same. Validate her new strategies: "It's a great idea to check to see what others are doing. That will remind you to raise your hand."
- Offer positive messages on the student's efforts. If the student did not have success one day, ask about it in a nonthreatening way:

  - "What went wrong today? How are you going to handle it tomorrow?"
  - "Can I help you in any way?"
  - Do not accept excuses. If she blames someone else or offers another excuse, simply say, "Bummer. What will you do about that tomorrow?" Do not accept the student's problem. As Jim Fay says, "Every time you make a student's problem your problem, you have denied him an opportunity to be successful in finding a solution" (Fay & Funk, 1995, p. 132).

- Set new goals for the next day. Continue until the new behavior is in place. Withdraw prompts and cues gradually. Check with student on this: "Can you remember without reminders from me?"

Throughout this process, use positive feedback that links effort to success. The student must see that her behavior is under her control. Her success here, especially when she attributes it to her own effort, establishes positive success expectations for the next behavior she needs to change. Typically, students who need this kind of individual plan have multiple misbehaviors they need to correct.

Individual Intervention Plan Tips

- Work on one behavior at a time.
- Start with the behavior that is either a safety issue, the most disruptive, or drives you the craziest.
- Make very specific the behavior to correct. For example, say "Raise your hand when you want to talk" rather than "Behave appropriately."
- When working on one behavior, ignore (as much as possible) other misbehaviors. Keep focused on the identified objective. Give feedback only on the targeted behavior.
- Provide no extrinsic rewards unless they are absolutely necessary; focus on improvement in behavior as reflected in data. Give feedback that attributes effort, or the acquisition of new strategies, for the success. Reinforce *progress,* not just perfection.

- Use no consequences at first, and do not include them in the plan. If the student slips a day (and he or she will!) discuss what went wrong and what the student will do differently tomorrow. Follow the hierarchy of reinforcers *within* the intervention plan. You may have to go to demands and consequences, but not until you have tried negative reinforcers.

- This is a plan to change behavior, not punish it. Reteach, practice, and give feedback on the student's performance. You and the student are working as a team. The mode is one of problem solving, "We have a problem we need to solve. Let's talk about it. I will support you any way I can." This goes a very long way in preventing power struggles. It is very difficult for a student to have a power struggle with someone on *his* side!

- Often, going through this intervention process with a student changes the relationship the two of you have. I have frequently seen a student develop great trust and respect for the teacher as they work through this together. The student sees the teacher as a caring person who is there to help. Attention is received (which often is what the student seeks) and that alone turns the relationship—and the behavior—around.

Outside Referrals

There are two kinds of outside referrals (Levin & Shanken-Kaye, 1996): on-site resources (e.g., school psychologist or principal) and outside professionals.

School Psychologist, Principal, or On-Site Resource Person

You are involved in this intervention, but now the decisions are made as a group. The parents are definitely involved at this stage, if not before. It is a teacher decision when to bring parents in. It is my personal opinion that we often call in the parents so quickly that the student can pass the responsibility for his behavior right on to them. I prefer trying to work it out between the teacher and the student. The student needs to have the opportunity to solve the problem on his or her own. I might say something like, "Do you think you and I can work this out, or do you want to call your parents in for a meeting?" If the student wants to work on his or her own, I respond, "I'm sure we can solve this problem together. If we can't, we can call your mom in later." This lets the student know I am confident in his or her problem-solving ability. The student also knows I won't go for long without contacting the parents! I want to add here that many schools have the rule that parents are called at the first incidence of misbehavior. I recommend that you check with your administrator about the policy at your site.

Outside Professional

This is the last step on the hierarchy because it is the only intervention that the teacher does not participate in or implement in the classroom. This intervention is not a direct interaction between the teacher and the student.

Section Summary

The goal of Section 2, as stated in the introduction, is to discuss how to establish and maintain a learning environment that is consistent with the roles students will assume in their schools now and in their world later. Their world will be one that values innovation, initiative, individuality, and self-control, and our classrooms need to reflect the expectations of this new century. Schooling is different for our students in the information age. It is built on principles of mutual respect and caring, and it is focused on teaching students responsibility and self-discipline.

Schooling is different for the 21st-century teacher as well. We no longer control our students; we teach them to control themselves. The classroom climate is warm and friendly. Leadership is shared between the teacher and students. We function as a learning community where we cooperate, not compete—where we coach, teach, guide, and persuade, rather than insist and demand. Our jobs as teachers are challenging and exciting. We are supremely important in the life of a child, and the difference we make is astounding. We can only control our own behavior, but we have tremendous power to influence our students. Don't forget Henry Adams's wise words: "A teacher affects eternity; you never know where your influence stops."

Instructional Strategies

Ginny Hoover

SECTION **THREE**

Implementing Effective Instructional Strategies

Even when classes are small and students are motivated, it is necessary for teacher both to be truly knowledgeable and to know how to transmit the desired or required knowledge to students.
—Howard Gardner (1991, p. 141)

Many teachers are introduced to their new teaching assignment in a brief interview with the principal, presented the keys to their classroom, and given an orientation to the building. They are issued a copy of the mandated curriculum and shown the available instructional resources. But, it is the teacher's responsibility to figure out how to use the resources and choose strategies to teach the curriculum to every student to the appropriate depth.

Depending on your school, district, and state, the required curriculum must be consulted to understand the material to be covered and the required depth of understanding. Accountability alone makes it mandatory that teachers know and understand state requirements and the tools used to assess students. Once the curriculum has been reviewed, strategies can be considered.

Knowledge of the students' abilities and skill levels along with an understanding of students' prior knowledge helps determine the appropriate strategy. If a class has many students reading below their grade level, it is a poor choice of strategies to assign silent reading of the chapters. That doesn't mean that reading assignments are not appropriate, but it does mean that lengthy, hard-to-understand sections shouldn't be assigned, because students are not likely to achieve acceptable levels of understanding.

Other considerations are the limitations and accommodations necessary for the inclusion of special education students into the classroom. The types of accommodations necessary are based on the types of disabilities children have and whether the teacher is given extra support to work with these children.

Time constraints make a critical difference in whether a strategy can be used successfully. In situations where there are a large number of curriculum objectives to cover in a short time span, teachers may have to forgo strategies that are time consuming.

Access to necessary materials must be considered when strategies are chosen. Scarcity of materials may make it necessary to work in a rotation plan or to share supplies, making group work a necessity. Some strategies might not be possible at all because of material limitations.

Implementation of a strategy should include explicit instructions from the teacher: "This is what I want to see." Students do not automatically realize what a teacher expects. After a strategy has been effectively implemented in the classroom several times, students need less direction in future applications.

There are some strategies that require behind-the-scenes planning. For example, selecting students to work together requires preplanning. The better these up-front tasks are done, the easier the strategy is to implement.

A plan to assess the success of the strategy implemented is an essential element in effective teaching. Spot checks can be something as simple as evaluating a student's oral explanation of information learned or giving a quick quiz. Monitor what is happening and be ready to adjust the teaching plan.

Once a strategy has been implemented, it is essential that the teacher do on-the-spot monitoring in order to ensure that all students understand their role in its success. When weaknesses are spotted, a teacher can provide interventions or observe until the student is on the right track. Interventions provided by the teacher are crucial to the success of each strategy and to helping students achieve the ultimate goal of learning.

Quality instruction is something educators have tried to define, refine, and implement successfully throughout history. When teachers recognize potential in a new strategy, they do not throw out sound strategies they already use. Because good teaching practices are not fads, effective teachers add new strategies to their bag of tricks and pull out what is appropriate for the current lesson. At times, it is appropriate, even expedient, to implement several strategies at the same time and offer choices to the students.

In this book, strategies are categorized according to the number of participants involved—whole class, small group, pairs, and individuals. Some strategies are very structured, whereas others allow teachers and students some freedom. Knowledge of the unique characteristics of each strategy helps teachers make insightful choices. Understanding students and curriculum, choosing strategies wisely, implementing strategies with explicit instructions, and monitoring and adjusting are the keys to effective instruction.

In her book *The Model: Integrated Thematic Instruction* (1994), Susan Kovalik stated:

We are born virtual learning machines. We become our environment and our brains are a recording of what we have done, and where we have been literally becomes who we are. Humans are born with a keen drive to understand and act upon their world. When information is identified by it as "meaningful," it jumps into high gear. (p. 51)

Our classroom strategies facilitate that drive to learn.

—Ginny Hoover

10 Whole-Class Strategies

Learning and teaching should not stand on opposite banks and just watch the river flow by; instead, they should embark together on a journey down the water. Through an active, reciprocal exchange, teaching can strengthen learning how to learn.
—Loris Malaguzzi (Edwards, 1993, p. 56)

The advantages of presenting instruction to the whole class are attractive to many teachers. Whole-class strategies generally require less preparation time and instruction time. Typical whole-class strategies include lecture, discussion, debate, teacher demonstrations, and giving directions.

Lecture

Lecture is generally defined as the verbal imparting of knowledge. Combining lectures with other strategies may enhance them. They are teacher-centered and, therefore, allow for greater teacher control. Lecturing places the teacher in the role of an "expert" sharing knowledge with students. It is often used to

- Provide basic knowledge needed for future activities.
- Present an overview of knowledge important for students to learn.
- Function as a catalyst for the students' learning endeavors.

Lectures allow the teacher to present a large amount of information efficiently. Figure 10.1 is a guide to help you make preparations for a lecture and consider some of the problems and disadvantages of the lecture strategy.

Figure 10.1
Lecture Planning at a Glance

Making Preparations	Problems and Disadvantages
• Make or collect visuals (transparencies, posters, computer presentations) to support main points. • Develop supports for note taking (incomplete outlines, fill in the blanks, audiotapes). • Plan stops and starts (activities with interaction). • Write questions to guide high-level thinking. • Develop a plan to assess level of student understanding.	• Possible listening-skills deficiencies or short attention spans • Teacher's lecture skills • Level of student preparedness— student involvement and prior knowledge • Limited student interaction with the content • Presentation of limited point of view

Making Preparations

Planning is the key to delivering a successful lecture. Lecturers need at least a brief outline. It is important to keep in mind that successful lectures are built around a few main points. The outline should include the following:

- Purpose and objectives for learning outcomes
- Important details or points
- Examples and illustrations to support each main point
- Summary
- Assessment plan

A well-planned framework is particularly helpful to teachers who must present the same lecture multiple times. The outline serves as a checklist to ensure completeness each time the lecture is given.

Appropriate Topics

Figure 10.2 gives examples of topics that are appropriate for the lecture strategy and those that are not.

Figure 10.2
Lecture Application Examples

Appropriate Application of Lecture	Less-Effective Application of Lecture
Mathematics: Present the problem-solving method and show examples of successful use.	**Mathematics:** Application of the problem-solving method (more effective in a student-centered strategy)
Communications: Introduce a piece of literature, such as a novel.	**Communications:** Teaching the parts of speech (requires a high level of student participation and interaction with teacher)
Science: Present an overview of a science unit, including main topics, expected learning, and a challenge to explore.	**Science:** Topics requiring detailed information (best in written form, such as learning the symbols for the elements)

Visuals

Although lecture is primarily verbal, combining it with other strategies enhances its value. Visuals such as transparencies, posters, and computer presentations increase students' levels of comprehension of material presented in a lecture.

Supports for Note-Taking

Another useful strategy is providing handouts. These might take the form of incomplete outlines or fill-in-the-blank statements completed with information presented in the lecture. Either type of handout can easily be made from the teacher's lecture outline. These tools require students to listen carefully for key information and fill in the missing parts. They also serve to accommodate students needing additional assistance (e.g., special education and at-risk students). Consider making audiotapes of your lecture for students who have even greater difficulties learning by listening so that the students have multiple opportunities to listen.

Stop and Start Times and Questioning

Stop and start times are the points of greatest learning. Therefore, to increase the value of a lecture, plan quick activities for a break from the lecture. During this time students can complete a short activity, such as discussing a teacher-provided question, sharing the most important facts or information presented, or using information provided to solve a problem. The teacher then brings the group back together, at which time students might share the results of the quick activity before the lecture is resumed.

Problem: Students are yawning, and their eyes have that glossed-over appearance. Don't you recall lectures that put you to sleep? *Solution:* Middle school students don't even try to disguise their boredom; their body language is the easiest to read. Don't wait for a planned break. Stop. Initiate a quick activity and then resume your lecture.

Assessment

It is important to determine the effectiveness of your lecture. Some instructors use a quick quiz. Although this provides some feedback, a quiz does not measure the value of the students' lecture notes. Having students use their notes as a basis for additional activities provides an opportunity for application of the new knowledge.

Problems and Disadvantages

Listening Skills

The listening skills and attention spans of students for lecture purposes cannot be ignored. Johnstone and Percival (1976) found that an adult's attention span is between 15 and 20 minutes. In addition, they note that the first instance of "downtime" occurs 3 to 5 minutes into the lecture, followed by another at the 10- to 18-minute mark. The length of quality attention time becomes shorter as lectures progress. (Please note that these findings refer strictly to lectures without visuals or stop/start times, and that the attention spans of elementary and middle-school students are even shorter than those of adults.)

Use the following questions to help you decide whether to choose the lecture strategy and, if so, how to prepare students for learning via a lecture:

- Do your students have good listening skills?
- How long can your students listen effectively?
- Do your students have acceptable note-taking skills?
- Are your students comfortable asking questions in front of their peers?

Based on the assessment of your students' skills, you may decide to provide some tutoring before you use lecture as an effective strategy.

Lecture Skills

Another important factor is the speaking skill of the teacher. Analyze your ability to lecture by considering these questions:

- Do you speak clearly with expression and enthusiasm?
- Do you use gestures to emphasize important points?
- Do you make eye contact?

Your body language and the volume and pitch of your speech help students identify important points. If lecturing is difficult for you, practice delivering your lecture in front of a mirror or recording it on a tape recorder. Listen to the audio-tapes and use them to identify ways to improve your lecture skills.

Student Preparedness

The following questions and answers help you identify other problems that can impact the effectiveness of a lecture and provide hints on how to address these problems.

What is the students' prior knowledge about this topic? It is imperative that teachers understand students' prior knowledge about the topic of the lecture. A lecture should begin on a firm foundation of prior knowledge and expand from there. One effective way to build a foundation for the topic is to ask students either to write or discuss what they already know about the topic and what they would like to learn about it.

What can be done to minimize passive learning? The stop and start activities designed for interaction and application support active learning. Lecturers need to make maximum use of these interaction opportunities by carefully planning quick activities and timing them to match students' attention spans. Student involvement increases each student's level of concern, resulting in greater efforts at listening and providing opportunity for interaction with the content of the lecture.

Point of View

When appropriate, various points of view should be included in the lecture. An effective way to do this is to present one point of view in the lecture and then ask students to generate other possible points of view.

Conclusion

Lecturing is a skill. It can be refined to an art. I had a college professor whose lectures were like soliloquies—performances that made time pass so quickly that we were amazed when the bell rang to signal the end of class. On the other hand, I had another college professor who spoke in monotones. He droned on for the full period with no chance for discussion or student interaction. The most exciting part of the class was watching his annoying habit of walking his fingers up the back of his head and then scratching his bald head multiple times during a lecture. Time crawled. What a waste!

It is important to be a well-prepared lecturer. To do less is a misuse of time on task. However, what if, in spite of your planning and preparations, your lecture is not working? That spaced-out look on the faces of students makes it obvious that their attention has wandered. It is time to insert a stop and start time requiring student input and activity. Ask questions such as, "What don't you understand?" and,

"Is this something you already know?" to determine whether to continue the lecture or shift to another strategy. Don't continue with a strategy that is failing. Identify the problem, solve it, and move forward either to continue the lecture or switch to another strategy. Lecturing is a valuable strategy only if it helps students accomplish the objectives of the lesson!

Discussion

Discussion focuses on interactions. Participants are allowed to express their knowledge, understandings, and opinions on a topic. It is a student-centered strategy in which teachers assume the role of facilitator, and students become interactive participants. Student participation promotes active learning and greater student accountability because students must share their knowledge.

Figure 10.3 is a guide to help you make preparations for a discussion and consider some of the problems and disadvantages of the discussion strategy.

Figure 10.3
Discussion Planning at a Glance

Making Preparations	Problems and Disadvantages
• Assure that students have sufficient prior knowledge of the topic. • Select a topic appropriate for discussion. • Create, teach, and enforce guidelines for quality discussions. • Ensure that each student has an equal opportunity to be involved in the discussion. • Develop questions to prompt and guide discussions. • Plan a culminating or summarizing activity.	• Difficult to guarantee full student participation • Difficult to keep students focused on topic • Difficult for teacher to know whether to intervene • Students' lack of prior knowledge or depth of understanding of topic

Making Preparations

Sufficient Prior Knowledge
Using discussion as a strategy involves knowing the abilities of each student. Because discussion is a student-centered strategy, success depends on the readiness of the students. The students' depth of knowledge of the topic is a critical variable

in determining whether the discussion strategy will be effective. For example, a discussion is effective following a period of study on the topic. This preparation makes it more likely that students can discuss the topic intelligently.

Appropriate Topics

When choosing a topic for discussion, consider its grade and age appropriateness as well as the students' abilities to understand the topic and participate in a discussion. Curriculum guides are valuable resources for discussion topic options.

Figure 10.4 gives examples of topics that are appropriate for the discussion strategy and those that are not.

Figure 10.4
Discussion Application Examples

Appropriate Application of Discussion	**Less-Effective Application of Discussion**
Mathematics: Find solutions to open-ended problems.	**Mathematics:** Learn how to do a mathematical procedure (requires a more linear approach).
Communications: Share personal reflections about a piece of literature.	**Communications:** Answer questions on a literature piece that require specific answers (no point to discuss as answers are clear cut).
Science: Share experiment results and their ramifications; consequences of choices.	**Science:** Learn the parts of a plant (text is a better source and working within a small group or partnership).

Discussion Guidelines

Preparing students to participate in discussions is essential. Decide if you want open discussions or restricted ones that require the raising of hands. Model and practice the rules for classroom discussions. Role-play different situations and identify appropriate and inappropriate responses to help students understand and respect the principles of quality discussions. As you begin to implement discussions in your classroom, stop the discussion if students ignore the rules. Ask students to modify their behavior to meet the predefined rules and then return to the discussion. When rules are disregarded, discussions may turn into aimless, chaotic conversations without educational benefit.

Problem: The discussion is out of control. It is no longer meeting the needs of the curriculum. *Solution:* Monitor and adjust. Don't be hesitant about changing what is not working. Out-of-control discussions yield little in the way of quality results. Primary students easily jump to unrelated topics, but the positive side is that with a few teacher comments they can be easily guided back to the topic!

Guiding Discussions with Questioning

One major issue in implementing classroom discussions is assuring that all students participate and that a few students do not dominate the discussion. Addressing teacher-directed questions or comments to inactive discussion participants may solve part of the problem, but it may also be necessary to set rules that limit the number of times a student can speak or to simply ask the student dominating the discussion to become a listener for a period of the time. Good preparation should include development of critical thinking questions to help guide the discussion through rough times.

Culminating or Summarizing

Summarizing activities enhance the value of a discussion. One possible activity involves having students summarize the content with teacher guidance. Another option is to have each student quickly share one idea from the discussion. The teacher then guides students in prioritizing the list. Plan for a culminating or summarizing activity to assess the quality of understanding developed by the discussion. If this assessment reveals a weakness in the students' overall level of knowledge, you may need to present this same lesson using another strategy.

Problems and Disadvantages

Level of Participation

Quality discussions depend on knowledgeable student interaction. It is easy to overlook uninvolved students. Tally sheets are one way to monitor student participation; use a class roster to help with these. When it becomes apparent that some students aren't involved, the teacher needs to decide on a course of action. Some students are naturally quieter than others and prefer not to talk in front of class. Are there times when lack of active participation should be allowed? Teachers know their students best, and lack of participation is an option for some students. Having those inactive students jot down what they learned can support passive participation. If that option is allowed, it should be given as a choice at the beginning of the discussion. However, nonparticipation because of student inattention should not be tolerated.

Staying on Topic

How does a teacher monitor a discussion so that students don't wander to tangential topics that arise in the discussion? Teaching students to self-monitor is a choice. Again, role-playing is helpful for training. When students understand the concept, they can help monitor the discussion.

Teacher Interventions

When discussions run off topic, teachers may also choose to interject a phrase as simple as "off topic" to guide older students. Subtle teacher interventions in the lower grades are less disruptive to the flow of discussion. How often a teacher has to intervene may be directly related to the amount of training done before the discussion strategy is used.

Misjudging Prior Knowledge

It may become apparent that students don't have a sufficient frame of reference to participate in a successful discussion. Bluffing will not make up for lack of knowledge. It is necessary in these cases to step back, build a firm foundation of knowledge, and then try the discussion again. It is possible for a teacher to misjudge the depth of students' prior knowledge. Acknowledge the error, discontinue the discussion, and initiate an alternative activity.

Conclusion

The discussion of the life cycles of skunks and turtles is flowing smoothly. With a look of genuine eagerness, a child offers, "My dog loves to play with turtles." Ignore this comment, and the discussion immediately turns to pets. Staying on the topic is the greatest challenge for students and, therefore, also for teachers.

Some of my middle-schoolers were at times tough to train. With one class I had to stop discussions that were off topic and switch to an alternative activity. After guiding them to realize that the rules are always followed, one student said, "Mrs. Hoover, that was interesting today. Why haven't we done this before? Could we do this again?" They finally realized that the quality of discussions improved when reasonable guidelines were followed. Even though I had taught the guidelines, I also had to prove I would enforce them.

The quality of discussion is also dependent on classroom management. If the teacher's control is weak, the possibility of a quality discussion is lessened. Good discussions require good classroom management, enforced guidelines, and adequate student preparation for the topic.

Debate

Classroom debates are based on controversial issues—issues that have pros and cons. Debates are student-centered; teachers take on the role of active facilitators. This strategy requires higher-level thinking. Students learn information about an issue or idea, take a position, relate their position to others, and defend it. Students must learn to listen to the opposing side and refute the arguments proposed in a convincing manner. They must learn to manipulate knowledge to appeal to both the factual and emotional needs of their audience.

Figure 10.5 is a guide to help you make preparations for a debate and consider some of the problems and disadvantages of the debate strategy.

Figure 10.5
Debate Planning at a Glance

Making Preparations	Problems and Disadvantages
• Select a quality debatable topic. • Ensure that students have in-depth knowledge of the debate topic. • Provide and enforce guidelines for debates. • Formulate a conclusion.	• Existing pro and con opinions already formed by some students • Inappropriate remarks made by students that lead to out-of-control emotions • Need for teacher to decide when intervention is appropriate • Level of respect for opinions of classmates

Making Preparations

Appropriate Topics

What constitutes a quality debate topic? What topic is appropriate for certain grade levels? Are there topics not appropriate for certain communities? Consider these questions as you select a debate topic. A good source of topics is your grade-level curriculum guide. Successful debates depend on students' abilities to understand the topic and to approach it with an attitude of intellectual curiosity rather than strong emotional reactions.

Figure 10.6 gives examples of topics that are appropriate for the debate strategy and those that are not.

Figure 10.6
Debate Application Examples

Appropriate Application of Debate	Less-Effective Application of Debate
Science: Debate biological advancements in medicine—such as genetic research.	**Science:** Situations that have only one possible solution (no debate issue)
Communications: Debate a controversial issue based on an expository piece.	**Communications:** Application of grammar rules (no debate issue)
Social Studies: Debate any appropriate social problem or issue.	**Social Studies:** Historical event (debate won't change history but if about if the right choice was made—that would be debatable)

In-Depth Knowledge

In order to debate, students must have a command of the knowledge regarding the topic. Before considering the debate strategy, plan to build a foundation of general knowledge. Once that knowledge has been acquired, opinions can be formed. Those opinions must be supported by facts, and the facts must be sorted to support a "for" or "against" position.

What about emotional pleas? How much emotion is acceptable in debates? Think of emotional pleas as a seasoning—a dash is enough. The strongest argument is based on facts and on the ability to manipulate facts to support a position.

Debate in a classroom can take different forms. Once students have a foundation of knowledge, simply opening up a controversial topic for discussion provides an opportunity to debate. Because there are no clear-cut sides in this type of debate, converting others to a position is easier because positions are not yet set.

In a more formal approach to classroom debate, a teacher might divide the classroom into "for" and "against" groups. Again, it is important to provide a basic foundation of knowledge, or an opportunity to do research to develop the knowledge. Assign students to plan arguments. An argument includes a defined position, facts to support the position, acknowledgment of and plans to refute the opposing position and a plea for support.

In both informal and formal forms of debate, students are exercising higher levels of thinking. There is a higher level of retention using the debate strategy because knowledge is applied, discussed, debated, and reviewed.

Remind students of the key elements of a debate: debatable topic; facts, facts, facts; a little emotional appeal; and a well-stated plea at the end. High school students tend either to distance themselves or become too emotional. They'll need guidance to find middle ground.

Guidelines

Guidelines for debate must be reviewed before a debate, and should include the following:

- How students share—show of hands, presentation of ideas, taking turns, or open debate
- Need to respect everyone's opinion—learning to agree to disagree
- Amount and type of preparation expected
- Monitoring style of teacher—how the teacher responds if the debate gets out of control or off track
- Type of concluding activity—how the students or teacher will summarize to ensure maximum application of knowledge

Concluding Activity

The debate should be stopped before the end of class for a summarizing or concluding activity. This doesn't mean that one side must "win." The concluding activity might be something as simple as a summary from both sides. Some classes might even want to vote on which side presented the best argument. Whatever the final activity used, the end result is that students must review what has been said and decide for themselves how effectively the arguments were presented. This further cements the knowledge shared.

Problems and Disadvantages

Preformed Opinions
A teacher carefully plans a debate activity only to learn that no one wants to be on the "for" or "against" team. Instead of a debatable topic, the class holds a unified opinion. This happens. Best alternative? Change your strategy for this topic or find another topic to debate. Most forced sides don't enter the debate with enthusiasm and sincerity. There are exceptions, but why push it? It is easy to move into a discussion strategy and discuss why students have taken a unified position on the issue and explore the opposing position without debate.

Inappropriate Remarks
On the opposite side, some topics are particularly "hot." Opinions may be so drastic that students forget to respect those of others and make entirely inappropriate comments instead.

Teacher intervention. When the debate appears to get out of hand, the teacher should remind students to monitor how they say things before something cruel or inconsiderate is said. This can be done simply with a predetermined warning word said by the teacher, such as "respect," "self-monitor," or "careful." However, once something inappropriate has been said, damage control must be instituted. This is the reason that training in the debate format with less-controversial topics is helpful. Students learn that emotion can only be used with temperance.

Repect for others. Even if emotions are in check, students need to show respect for others. It's easy for students to write off opinions that are in opposition to their own as "dumb," "stupid," or "ridiculous." Learning to agree to disagree respectfully is a skill that many adults haven't mastered, but it is one that should be taught with debate.

Conclusion
"You're crazy," an angry debater responds. Emotions are out of control. Debate is a strategy that requires a high level of thought, but it is effective only when there is quality classroom management in place. Teachers must be active facilitators, monitoring for appropriate conduct until students have learned to function within the guidelines of classroom debate.

If debate seems ineffective, consider taking the following actions:

- Make a controversial statement to get the ball rolling again.
- Check for level of control by asking whether everyone feels comfortable expressing their opinions or whether it feels unsafe to make comments.
- Assess whether students have a sound foundation of knowledge or whether they are trying to bluff their way through the debate.

Teacher Demonstrations

Teacher demonstrations place the teacher in the role of "expert" providing knowledge or skills by demonstrating a step-by-step method. Demonstrations are a form of "show and tell." The following are some possible reasons teachers choose the demonstration strategy:

- There is limited time or a scarcity of necessary materials.
- The goal of the lesson is to give students a pattern or procedure to follow, and a demonstration is an efficient way to do that.
- To limit student contact with dangerous materials by demonstrating proper usage.

Figure 10.7 is a guide to help you make preparations for a teacher demonstration and consider some of the problems and disadvantages of the demonstration strategy.

Figure 10.7
Teacher Demonstration Planning at a Glance

Making Preparations	**Problems and Disadvantages**
• Develop a plan for you to follow or establish a pattern for students to follow (consider a handout). • Gather materials or be sure they are easily accessible. • Practice the demonstration if it involves several steps, or if you have not done this demonstration previously.	• Room arrangement or space not adequate to allow all students a direct line of sight to the demonstration • Limited student involvement • Excessive amount of time required for set-up and clean-up

Making Preparations

Making Plans and Establishing a Pattern

The teacher's preparation depends on the purpose of the demonstration. If the purpose is to model good demonstration format, a plan should be developed, demonstrated, and shared with students. This plan should contain the desired actions and the order in which they are to be done, as well as any other requirements, such as visuals. Handouts that explain the demonstration pattern help students follow the process.

Other purposes for teacher demonstrations do not require student understanding of the presentation format. The purpose for these demonstrations is to show how to do something and to provide information to support the demonstration. In these cases, students take notes on what the teacher shares, not how the teacher shares.

Appropriate Topics

Figure 10.8 gives examples of topics that are appropriate for the demonstration strategy and those that are not.

Figure 10.8
Teacher Demonstration Application Examples

Appropriate Application of Demonstration	Less-Effective Application of Demonstration
Mathematics: Solve difficult math problems using manipulatives.	**Mathematics:** Modeling concepts for which students have already demonstrated mastery (not time efficient)
Communications: Make a graphic organizer to show relationships.	**Communications:** As an introductory activity (better comprehension as a culminating activity— for example, provide instruction on graphic organizer and then demonstrate its use)
Science: Model the use of the scientific method to test a hypothesis.	**Science:** Any topic for which students lack sufficient knowledge to understand the principles presented (wonderful demonstration no one can explain)

Gathering Materials

The key to successful demonstrations is advance planning. Demonstration materials need to be easily accessible. Check that all materials are in good working order

and that quantities are sufficient. Waiting until the last minute to round up materials is not wise!

Practicing

Practicing a demonstration before presenting it to the class might save embarrassing moments. This is particularly important for science demonstrations. Many times the demonstration might not yield the results you intend because of various factors (e.g., the quality of the materials, the lack of precise measuring devices, or malfunctioning equipment).

Problems and Disadvantages

Seeing the Demonstration

Students need a direct line of sight to the demonstration area. Sometimes you can use larger demonstration items (such as a large clock face to demonstrate how to compute elapsed time) so that students can see from a distance. Another solution is to film the demonstration using a video camera connected to a large-screen television. Position the television to provide a close-up view for students seated a distance away from the demonstration site. You can also help students follow the demonstration by using large posters showing illustrations of each step.

Limited Student Involvement

Because students are inactive in the demonstration process, it is vital to increase the level of involvement. Pausing and having a student review what has been done so far can do this. Quick assessments raise the level of concentration and increase student attention.

Preparation Time

One of the disadvantages of demonstration is the time needed to set up and clean up. Organization and preplanning will be helpful in reducing the time needed, as will training your students to assist with these tasks.

Conclusion

Imagine a teacher demonstrating stable air conditions by stacking two jars of water, one cold and one hot, and placing a piece of cardboard in between the stacked jars to separate the two types of water. The teacher plans to remove the cardboard without spilling the water or shaking the jars. As the teacher pulls on the cardboard, the top jar slides. The demonstration failed! Practice might have given the teacher the experience needed to avoid the mess of water spilling out of the jar and ruining the demonstration.

Recipe for failure: forget to organize materials, fail to practice the steps, and gamble on results. The eyes of your primary students are glued to your demonstration table, but you seem to have forgotten something. As quickly as you captured their attention, you will surely lose it because you were not prepared!

Because teacher demonstrations have few variables to consider, they have a high level of successful completion. The question to consider is, "Do they accomplish the learning goal?" If not, consider increasing the level of student involvement—by asking questions, requiring note taking, or other interactions—or providing equal visual opportunities for all students by meeting the needs of those situated the furthest from the demonstration.

Providing Directions

Providing directions is teacher-centered and is one of the most common whole-group presentations. Giving efficient information on the how, what, where, and when of assignments and class activities makes everyone's lives easier. Providing directions isn't as much a teaching strategy as it is a teacher tool. Used effectively it paints a picture of how the assignment should look—what steps are necessary to complete the work and what the end product is.

Figure 10.9 is a guide to help you make preparations for giving good directions and consider some of the problems and disadvantages involved when giving directions.

Figure 10.9
Providing Directions Planning at a Glance

Making Preparations	Problems and Disadvantages
• Present a well-defined task with a specified method of assessment. • Provide both written and oral directions. • Engage every student's attention before giving the directions and be prepared to answer specific questions before and during the activity.	• Student confusion about what to do • Missing details in the directions or unclear • Lack of students' attention

Making Preparations

Well-Defined Tasks
An assignment should be a well-defined task! Students should know exactly what is to be done and how to do it. Of course, in assignments such as daily math work, the directions are simple: "Do the even problems on page 232. Show your work. Be prepared for a quiz tomorrow covering these math skills." This type of direction

follows classroom instruction. In addition to giving oral directions, jotting the information on the board or on an overhead transparency prevents confusion.

Instructions

If the assignment is a lengthy one, students benefit greatly from both oral directions and a written checklist of required components along with assessment information—including the rubrics or scoring guide if used.

Appropriate Topics

Figure 10.10 gives examples of topics that are appropriate for giving directions and those that are not.

Figure 10.10
Providing Directions Application Examples

Appropriate Application of Providing Directions	Less-Effective Application of Providing Directions

Social Studies/English: Research paper. Oral and written instructions (handouts) for research paper with opportunity for questions.
 	
Topics to address:
• Acceptable topics
• Required points to be covered
 	
Format:
• Note cards
• Works cited
• Length of paper
• What to be handed in
• Thesis statement
• Citing within the paper
 	
  Instructions defining what is required for English *or* what is required for social studies.
  Include rubrics or scoring guide—English may use rubrics different from the rubrics used in social studies.
	Social Studies/English: Research paper. "Write a research paper on the social studies topic of your choice."

Giving directions for lengthy assignments without preparation directly increases the amount of backtracking a teacher must do to repair the faulty work. Always be prepared to provide quality instructions or to respond to complaints and questions regarding the assignment. This is sound advice for all grades!

Engaging Student Attention and Being Prepared for Questions

Before starting to give detailed directions, be sure that you have students' attention. Allow them the opportunity to ask questions to clarify the assignment.

Problems and Disadvantages

Student Confusion

Even when teachers believe they have given quality directions, there are usually questions. It is tempting to write off students' concerns, but it is best to address them immediately—to welcome questions and provide answers. When it is evident that very few students have questions, talking individually to the few who do is a viable option.

Missing Details, Lack of Clarity

It is possible that, even with careful preparation in organizing the assignment, some details are missing or unclear. When this happens, write yourself a note to rectify the situation before giving the assignment again.

Lack of Student Attention

No matter how carefully you ask students for their attention as you give directions, some of them may well be off into a dream world of their own or somehow distracted by the actions of others. It happens—be prepared to deal with it.

Conclusion

"I don't understand," claims a student. "How could you not understand? I just spent 15 minutes going over every detail," responds the teacher. Sound familiar? This is why providing a written handout mirroring your oral directions is a helpful time-saver. Students can take notes on the handout and refer to them in the future. It won't stop all questions, but it definitely puts a dent in the number. In addition, a rubric or scoring guide helps students see how their work will be graded, which also helps guide them in completing the assignment. Lengthy assignments need careful planning.

Still having students question about how to do an assignment? Consider

- Organizing what is said and how it is written.
- Engaging the attention of every student before you begin giving directions.
- Updating handouts when flaws are found.

Summary

The strategies discussed in this chapter have common threads. The teacher needs to select the one that fits best, complete preparation for successful implementation, train students in appropriate conduct and response, implement the strategy, monitor for success during implementation, make adjustments as needed, and check student comprehension after completion.

Interestingly enough, the level of classroom management is quite varied. As the level of student involvement increases, so does the need for quality classroom management. Of course, anytime students are working with materials that might be dangerous, the level of management increases as well, and strategies that include "hot topics" require closer monitoring. At all times, students need a safe environment in which to make comments and ask questions.

The willingness to select strategies wisely; monitor, adjust, and change strategies when needed; and consistently check for quality of understanding are all options that enhance the teacher's effectiveness. Being flexible is the name of the game!

Additional Reading

If you are interested in learning more about whole-class instruction, consider reading the following:

Cummings, C. (2002). *Teaching makes a difference* (pp. 111–120). Edmonds, WA: Teaching. (This section of the book addresses the active participation of students.)

Gunter, M. A., Estes, T. H., & Schwab, J. H. (1999). *Instruction: A models approach* (3rd ed., pp. 279–280). Boston: Allyn & Bacon. (Information can be found here on the "think, pair, share" technique.)

Harmin, M. (1994). *Inspiring active learning* (pp. 23–48). Alexandria, VA: Association for Supervision and Curriculum Development. (The selected pages cover student involvement during lectures.)

11 Small-Group Strategies

Collaboration involves more than occasional cooperative learning activities; it means that students feel connected to their peers and that they experience the classroom as a safe, supportive community—not a place of isolation and certainly not a place where they must compete against one another.
—Alfie Kohn (1998, p. 157)

There are times when having students work in groups is the most effective strategy. There are many benefits derived from working together to achieve goals, such as completing a multitask project, learning a defined body of information, and sharing the work in researching a topic. Group work is time-consuming, requires excellent classroom management skills, and entails the challenge of obtaining a quality effort from each team member. Yet in the small-group setting, students have a greater opportunity for participation and the possibility of increased learning and retention.

One of the stumbling blocks to effective group work is ineffective classroom management. Without good management and organization, group work is a waste of valuable class time. To prevent failures in group work due to management, the following items need to be addressed:

- The way students move into groups and, if necessary, furniture rearrangement
- The amount of freedom in movement allowed
- The acceptable noise level
- The plan for solving in-group conflicts

In addition, the following possibilities for conflict need to be addressed:

- How division of labor is handled (the organization of students within the group)
- How an individual is accountable within a group
- How to deal with group members who are not completing assigned tasks
- How grading, if any, is done
- How the allotted time is divided
- When work is due

It is wise to practice or model acceptable group behaviors with a short task or activity before moving into any lengthy group task or assignment.

Cooperative Learning

Although there are a variety of models for cooperative learning, they are all similar in nature. Group formations include students of mixed abilities, ethnicities, and genders. The groups share a common goal of learning preselected material, working interdependently to attain mastery, and making sure that all group members successfully achieve the group goal. In cooperative learning, participants learn as a group in a noncompetitive environment but are assessed as individuals, with possible bonus points when all group members achieve positive results. One goal of this type of group work is to teach individuals how to attain similar goals independently.

Figure 11.1 is a guide to help you make preparations for cooperative learning and consider some of the problems and disadvantages of the cooperative learning strategy.

Making Preparations

Selecting Members of Each Group
A cooperative learning group is a slice of the classroom population. Generally, that means a teacher thinks about students' abilities, genders, and ethnicities to form each group. It is wise to keep students who have social issues with each other in separate groups. The strict form of cooperative learning requires that a student of high ability be available to tutor.

Figure 11.1
Cooperative Learning Planning at a Glance

Making Preparations	Problems and Disadvantages
• Select members of each group. • Define the task (acquiring knowledge). Teach skills of cooperative learning (coaching, mentoring, learning). • Provide necessary resources (flashcards, hand-outs, spelling lists). • List and teach rules. • Determine assessment tools (individual or limited group accountability—bonus points for success).	• Burden or stigma of being the high or low student of the group • Personality clashes • Lack of ownership within the group • Failure of a member to learn the material • Excessive social interaction

Defining the Task

The type of task to be accomplished is the acquisition of knowledge. In the lower grades, learning the spelling list, memorizing math facts, or identifying the parts of a flower are appropriate tasks. For older students, answering a set of questions and showing mastery of the material are appropriate. The task is teacher controlled. The information to be learned is carefully defined. The necessary materials to accomplish the task are provided by the teacher, and each group is to pursue the same result.

Teaching Cooperative Learning Skills

Within the group, there are defined jobs, such as materials handler, recorder, group leader, and so forth. Listing the expectations for each job in the groups is helpful in accomplishing the task. Teachers can assign the roles or allow group members to select the roles as part of the group process. Expediency may necessitate that the teacher assign the roles, but student choice gives students more ownership of the task at hand. Using role-play to show how the group should function may be helpful. As students refine their cooperative learning skills, teachers are less likely to have to spend time instructing students in appropriate group process and intervening to get students back on task.

Appropriate Topics

Figure 11.2 gives examples of appropriate and inappropriate topics for the cooperative group strategy.

Figure 11.2

Cooperative Learning Application Examples

Appropriate Application of Cooperative Learning	Less-Effective Application of Cooperative Learning
Mathematics: Learn and apply math formulas.	**Mathematics:** Solve open-ended story problems (appropriate as collaborative learning activity).
Communications: Master the list of spelling words.	**Communications:** Record definitions for a vocabulary list for a literature piece (best as individual activity for effective time usage).
Social Studies: Learn the rights listed in the Bill of Rights.	**Social Studies:** Complete a worksheet of matching exercises (a more appropriate task is to learn the answers after completing the worksheet).

Providing Needed Resources

It is essential to have the necessary materials available for group use. For instance, in lower grades if the task is to learn math facts, a list of the facts to be learned or flashcards should be available. In addition, the teacher might provide an assessment tool similar to the testing materials so that students can assess their skills and check their level of proficiency. In this way, students have a guide for knowing when they have accomplished the task.

In the upper grades if the task is to locate and learn the material as defined by the teacher, the teacher might provide an incomplete outline or fill-in-the-blank study guide to let the students know what knowledge is required. This way the majority of the time can be used for learning the material, not finding the answers or guessing at what is important. Also, a sample assessment tool is helpful in gauging the results or success of the study.

Listing Rules

Students need to know what is expected of them; unless teachers are willing to listen to dozens of "Johnny won't do his work," they need to give students tools for dealing with the dynamics of the group. In lower grades, teacher intervention may often be necessary, but in upper grades students should be gaining skills in dealing with problems within the group. Group grade bonuses often help motivate students to work together to learn. (For example, if all students in the group score an 80 percent or better, all receive a 10 percent bonus on their individual grades.) Ultimately, it may be necessary for the students to just ignore the defiant student

"Hey, we all made it! We get the bonus points!" Enthusiasm is shared when success is achieved using this strategy—the very same words could easily be heard from students of elementary through high school.

and move forward, so that their own learning and grades are not affected by the actions or lack of action on the part of a group member. There must be a "back door" to allow groups to deal with the student who refuses to do the work. There are times when the best teacher cannot motivate a student to learn. It isn't reasonable to hold students to a higher standard than the teacher can accomplish.

Determine Assessment Tools

Students need to know how they are assessed on the group's learning objective. As previously mentioned, students also benefit from having a sample test similar to the final test. With the math facts, it might be a timed fact test. In science, it might be a fill-in-the-blank diagram of a flower.

As the group works together to learn the information, the opportunity for bonus points shouldn't be used to the extent that if one student fails to meet the goal of the group then everyone else in the group is angry or disappointed with the failing student. There is a limit to what is acceptable in peer pressure. The stress of accountability should be on individual success based on cooperation within the group.

Problems and Disadvantages

Burden of Being the High or Low Student

When cooperative learning is used extensively in the classroom, the students who are likeliest to complain are those who are designated high or low within a group. Even though these positions are not advertised, all the students in the group know their standing within the group. The high-designated student may complain about having to be responsible for others' learning when he already knows the answers. The low-designated student has problems with members of the group being disappointed that she has not learned the information within the allotted time (children are often not tactful when that happens). The careful selection of tasks that even lower-level students can master helps alleviate this problem.

Personality Clashes

Because the students are being asked to learn information in an allotted time, there is built-in stress. Stressful situations sometimes bring out the worst in students, and students who normally get along in less-stressful situations may strike out in frustration. When this happens, the success of a cooperative learning group becomes less likely. Task definition may need to be reconsidered for difficulty and clarity. The following questions can help you identify problem areas:

- Are clashes within the group due to social problems or to stress?

- Are students required to accomplish too much or too little in the allotted time?
- Are students required to learn material beyond the ability of some members of the group?
- Are students being too pressured into succeeding?

Knowing the cause of the disruptions in learning may help you find a solution.

Lack of Ownership Within the Group

When there are students who don't buy into the "working together to complete a task" strategy, there may be a lack of ownership. Students may demonstrate this lack of ownership by responding with one of the following behaviors:

- Using an attention-getting device
- Displaying a negative attitude about working with others
- Exhibiting a feeling of insecurity in the group
- Demonstrating that the learning strategy is not effective for them

If one student continues to opt out of group work by not participating, perhaps he needs an alternative choice for learning the material.

Failure of a Member to Learn

When a student fails to learn the material for any reason, that may cause the group to feel they have failed. The teacher must decide how to deal with negative feelings caused by failure of one student in the group to succeed, especially if that member tried very hard and still failed. Peer disappointment and anger may be harder for a student to accept than teacher responses to the same situation. This is a good time to monitor and adjust anything in the definition of the task that might have made it too hard for the low-performing student to accomplish.

Excessive Social Interaction

When the group is down to one person who doesn't know the information, the two or more not actively involved in the teaching and learning process wrestle with the temptation of social conversation. Noise levels may increase when this happens, and the teacher must decide on an action so time on task is not lost.

Conclusion

Cooperative learning is an excellent teaching strategy to help all students acquire basic knowledge. The disadvantage in overuse of cooperative learning is the displeasure voiced by high and low students within the group who bear the most responsibility for the success of the group. So this strategy works best when incorporated in a classroom with a variety of strategies. I know of one school that adopted the strategy as part of a schoolwide program. Teachers from that district shared how ineffective it had been as an everyday strategy. If you use cooperative learning in your classroom, remember two good guidelines: don't overdo the strategy, and *carefully select tasks* so that all have the possibility of being successful.

Collaborative Learning

Collaborative learning requires students to work together, but the outcome is generally more open-ended. Individual responsibility for learning is greater in a collaborative setting. The group goals are different from the goals of cooperative learning. There is less teacher input and greater student freedom to explore learning. The teacher defines the task, but the group decides how to approach the task and produce an end product. The role of the teacher becomes more that of a facilitator. The goal of collaborative work is to learn by cooperation, interaction, research, and task completion.

Collaborative learning is often considered synonymous with cooperative learning. For the purpose of sharing effective strategies, the definitions for cooperative and collaborative learning already provided are used to address preparation for different types of activities.

Figure 11.3 is a guide to help you make preparations for collaborative groups and consider some of the problems and disadvantages of the strategy.

Figure 11.3
Collaboration Learning Planning at a Glance

Making Preparations	Problems and Disadvantages
• Select members of each group. • Keep in mind the task to be accomplished. • Define the task with expectations for results (the freedom to acquire knowledge and apply it). • Provide rubrics, if used. • List rules. • Determine assessment (prefer individual accountability).	• Less structured learning, so students must be more responsible • Classroom management demands • Availability of materials • Interacting with students without a definite pattern of action • Excessive social interaction by group members

Making Preparations

Selecting Members of Each Group

Keeping in mind the task to be accomplished, grouping for collaborative learning allows for choices—ones that best fit the defined task. One way to group is to have a skills grouping (leader, researcher, artist, follower, and so forth). For some group work, people with like skills, such as those with similar learning styles, might be a better choice. Students who have social ties and good working relationships might also be used to form a group. The teacher is free to select group members based on what works best for the particular class and the task to be performed.

Defining the Task with Expectations for Results and Rubrics

This type of group work allows the freedom to acquire knowledge through students' efforts and to apply the knowledge as defined by the teacher. In cooperative learning, the goal is that a specific body of knowledge is mastered. In collaborative learning, the results are unique to the group, and results of the work are assessed in a method predetermined by the teacher. It may be that students report back to the class what they have learned or perhaps provide a quick written summary of the information learned. This individual summary of information that is compiled later for the group becomes the basis for individual assessment.

When defining the task, the teacher provides the subject, defines the parameters for accomplishing the work, and describes appropriate resources to consult (e.g., school library and the Internet). It is not necessary for the teacher to provide all resources, but just guidance in what is expected (e.g., primary and secondary resources). The teacher's directions should include time constraints, final due dates, and (if needed) a time line showing intermediate deadlines. In addition, if rubrics are used to evaluate, then they should be included when defining the task.

Equalizing task labor within a collaborative group is a challenge. In a group of three, all students might evaluate materials for relevant facts. Then, one student might sort out the most important facts from the group research, another might organize the information for the response for the class, and the third might be responsible for developing a way of reporting to the class. At each stage the students not responsible for the task become the assistants. When the teacher presents expectations to the class, a model explaining labor division may prevent group disgruntlement. Older students experienced in group work may prefer to make the task assignments themselves. In this case, knowing the class and their experience with group work helps in knowing how detailed the teacher's direction must be.

Appropriate Topics

Figure 11.4 gives examples of appropriate and inappropriate topics for the collaborative group strategy.

Figure 11.4
Collaborative Learning Application Examples

Appropriate Application of Collaborative Learning	Less-Effective Application of Collaborative Learning
Mathematics: Solve open-ended math problems.	**Mathematics:** Learn math facts (cooperative learning activity).
Communications: Identify an issue in a literature piece and provide the pros and cons.	**Communications:** Answer recall-level questions about a literature piece (partnerships, loosely formed groups, or individuals can do this more time efficiently).
Science: Analyze the validity of the results of an experiment.	**Science:** Learn the meaning of science vocabulary terms (cooperative learning activity or partnerships are more effective).

Listing Rules

Many of the rules established for one kind of group work also apply to other types of groups (such as acceptable talking volume, freedom of movement around the classroom, and so forth). However, one additional rule for collaborative groups is needed to describe movement between rooms (e.g., library and computer rooms). Students also need to know the correct procedure for dealing with group members who do not fulfill their responsibilities. These procedures should apply both to students who are reluctant to work and to students who are absent due to illness, athletic events, and so forth. One option for dealing with these situations is to instruct the group to divide the absent classmate's work among the other group members. The absent classmate is then given an alternative assignment as makeup work.

Determining Assessment: Individual Accountability

A variety of assessment options are possible. A good choice is individual accountability for learning the information shared by the groups. For best results, students should know what type of assessment tool will be used and how it will be scored (e.g., rubrics with percentage-point scores).

Problems and Disadvantages

Less Structured Learning and Greater Need for Student Responsibility

Collaborative learning isn't accomplished in an environment that requires both students to keep their feet flat on the floor and eyes straight ahead and to follow the teacher's directions exactly. Rather, teachers are facilitators; they move to the side. Once the teacher has defined the requirements of the group work, the students are expected to responsibly address the issues of performing the assignment. Identifying group roles (recorder, timer, group chairperson, noise supervisor, and so forth) may assist students in successfully completing the group assignment.

Classroom Management Needs

All group work requires a framework of management. The rules may vary according to the kind of group, but the basic rules apply. In addition, collaborative group work requires extra expectations to cover the additional freedom and responsibilities that are an integral part of the group activity. The following questions define these additional expectations and can help teachers anticipate possible problem areas:

- How do students obtain permission to go to the library for research?
- Do they go to the library individually or in a group, or is the group free to decide?
- How do students obtain the necessary materials for their class presentation (i.e., markers, posterboard, transparencies, computer presentation software, projector, and so forth)?
- How do students cope academically with a group member who is not doing his or her share of the work? (It is equally important to explain what is expected of the group when chunks of work will be missing if not completed by other members of the group.)

Availability of Materials

Students need to know what materials they need to complete the assignment. If students are expected to supply some of the materials, they need that information before they begin work. Teachers should address the following questions before they require students to supply materials:

- Are supplies (such as posterboard or markers) affordable for students?
- Are supplies easily found or obtained?
- Is there time to find the needed materials (i.e., do local stores have it in stock)?

If the teacher is to supply all or part of the materials, these questions should be addressed:

- Where can the supplies be found?

"I promise I can do this" are words that may tumble from the at-risk student who carefully selects tasks from the collaborative project description. And that's the advantage: the various gifts of students can be pooled to develop and refine the collaboration.

- How will they be distributed?
- Will there be replacements if something happens to the original materials—if the student who has materials is ill, for instance, or if the materials are damaged?

Learning to Interact Without a Definite Pattern of Action

Remember that cooperative learning focuses on learning a defined body of material, while collaborative learning requires multitasking and shared responsibility. When first using collaborative group work, students may struggle to interact in a productive way. There are choices to be made. If students are new to collaborative learning, additional time should be allowed for the decision making and organizing that comes naturally after experience. Because roles may be less defined, success depends on students' acceptance of responsibility and willingness to work together to achieve a goal.

Excessive Social Interaction

Whenever students have the opportunity to sit in small groups, the temptation to talk about what happened Saturday night is ever present. Although some positive social interaction is natural and even desirable, when it interferes with achieving the group goals, it becomes a problem. One way to slow this type of interaction is to make careful group selections—use the *divide and conquer* technique. If experience proves that when two to three students are placed together in the same group, more conversation than work is accomplished, then place the talkative students in separate groups. Another way to curb excessive social talking is for the teacher to circulate among the groups to monitor and advise. The proximity of the teacher works as a deterrent to poor choices for group behavior.

Conclusion

Collaborative learning provides an opportunity for students to work in a group to accomplish a defined task in less time than working alone. Students are exposed to other students' perspectives and ways of working. The cliché "two heads are better than one" is an apt description for collaborative learning. Whereas the individual voices in the group enrich the experiences, the multiple voices require compromise and negotiation. Group members must find consensus answers to these questions:

- What is important?
- What constitutes the best solution to the task?
- How should the group present their information so others can learn the information the group has so diligently compiled?

Collaborative learning skills are indeed part of real life. The working-within-the-group skills that are acquired are equally valuable or even more valuable than the end product. If you use collaborative learning in your classroom, you'll experience its value. At the same time realize that collaborative learning is time consuming, so it needs to be used wisely.

Project Groupings

Project groupings are used when the purpose of a group is to complete a task resulting in a product or presentation, such as one might do for science or social studies. Completing projects in the classroom has become a common teaching strategy in involving active learning. Projects are often time consuming, but there is an opportunity to apply knowledge in order to prove that students understand the lesson's concepts.

Figure 11.5 is a guide to help you make preparations for project groupings and consider some of the problems and disadvantages of the strategy.

Figure 11.5
Project Grouping Planning at a Glance

Making Preparations	**Problems and Disadvantages**
• Select groups according to task needs. • Define the task, including various responsibilities of people within the group, and provide rubric if used. • Gather materials or develop a plan for accessing materials. • Plan assessment.	• Management of materials • Unfair scoring on project because of member irresponsibility • Overachievers slowing down the process • Excessive social interaction

Making Preparations

Selecting Groups According to Task Needs
Defining the group task must precede selecting group members. Matching the task to the group makes it more likely that the group work will be successful. Low-conflict groupings are a good choice for this type of work, especially if the assignment is a long-term project. This grouping is based on selecting members who maintain good working relationships.

Another type of grouping is skill or ability groupings. For example, if the task is a project board for social studies that requires research, a teacher might include a quality researcher, an artist, a speaker, and a leader. For a science project, a group might include a quality researcher, an exact recorder of observations, an artist, and an organizer who is responsible for the materials and information. Although grouping students who share the same learning style can work, a mixed-skills or mixed-knowledge group is more effective. Random groupings, especially for long-term projects, are usually not successful. The possibility that some groups might have conflicting personalities or be lacking in necessary skills or knowledge is simply too great.

Defining the Task and the Responsibilities of Each Group Member

A project task should be well defined. Careful directions prevent later confusion and the need for reminders of the requirements. It is wise to give detailed written and verbal instructions accompanied by a checklist with deadlines to avoid this problem and, if used, provide the rubrics at this time. Instructions might include hints as to the types of responsibilities needed to complete the project (e.g., materials manager or organizer, leader, researcher). If the project is a science project with some risks, safety rules should be reviewed and included in print with directions. It is important that teachers visualize the project, consider possible stumbling blocks, and design appropriate solutions. By doing this, teachers save valuable class time.

Acquiring or Accessing Materials

Many teachers assign science projects and expect students to split the cost and purchase the display boards at the local store. If this strategy is to be successful, the teacher must consider these issues:

- Does the local supplier have enough of an inventory to meet the needs of the number of students doing such a project?
- Is the cost within the means of all students?
- If there is one classroom set of materials (such as magnets) that must be shared, are they available for use?
- If library research is required, has the library been reserved and has the librarian been informed of students' expectations?

Planning issues have the potential to make or break a project. In fact, deciding what materials are needed, whether they are available, and devising a reasonable plan for obtaining missing materials are musts. The planning list might include scheduling the library, providing information to the librarian, and scheduling the computer room (Internet access for research). It is important to list the necessary physical materials and to determine whether they are in the classroom or whether they must be borrowed or checked out from the school or district media and materials center. Students should have a list of materials they are expected to supply and know when they must be available to the group. Once these issues are addressed, the group work can begin.

Appropriate Topics

Figure 11.6 gives examples of appropriate and inappropriate topics for project groupings.

Figure 11.6
Project Grouping Application Examples

Appropriate Application of Project Type Groupings	Less-Effective Application of Project Type Grouping
Social Studies: Complete a historical project board and analysis paper.	**Social Studies:** Make a notebook of the chapter questions and vocabulary (not time efficient).
Science: Do experiments and demonstrations.	**Science:** Perform a science experiment from the book that includes the expected results (unless done as a model for future group work).

Planning Assessment

Because group project grades can be a source of controversy, *if there is a way to determine individual grades, that is the best choice.* For example, students might write their initials beside the defined tasks they completed, and their grades might depend on those identified tasks.

Problems and Disadvantages

Managing Materials

Projects tend to generate lots of stuff. If the classroom is cluttered, it is critical that the teacher find specific storage places. These excess materials may present safety hazards, destroy the aesthetics of the learning environment, and invite students to tamper with the materials. Teachers should assign or have the group choose one person to take responsibility for storing the group's materials.

That whiny complaint, "I can't find it. I know I put it here." In elementary school, the grievance may be followed by a splash of tears. It saves a lot of grief to have a place for everything and to plan time to carefully put away materials.

Unfair Scoring Due to Irresponsible Project Members

When a group works on a project, there is the possibility that a member of the group does not complete his or her share of the work. If the whole group is made to pay for the irresponsibility of one, that causes frustration and anger. If the whole group must do the missing work in order to receive a good grade, then does the person who did no work receive the group grade that the others earned? How a teacher deals with grading group work may make a big difference in the classroom atmosphere during the project and its ultimate success or lack thereof. Grading projects as a group is controversial because of the possibility that uneven contributions are made to the end result, and yet all group members receive the same grade. There is a possibility of breaking down the project into separate parts so the grades can be assigned per individual. That is the best option.

Overachievers Slowing Down the Process

It is possible that an overachiever may slow a group to the point that deadlines are not met and that may cost the group time and grief. Students who set unreasonable standards for everyone else to meet must be tempered (not everyone can reach such high standards). These overachievers may be less of a disruption if they know that their grade depends solely on their own work and not the work of the group. Students who have high standards have the right to set those high standards for themselves but not for others.

Excessive Social Interaction

As with collaborative learning, the project work format lends itself to excessive talking and social interaction. As students become more familiar with the teacher's standards, students will comply—but the temptation to talk and get off track is always there. Because the teacher working with project groups is no longer the teacher on stage, different responsibilities exist. Teachers must be willing to circulate and to use proximity to manage, monitor, and adjust. The checklist given with the assignment may help encourage on-task behavior because it breaks down the project into smaller pieces. If deadlines are included, it increases the level of concern and encourages forward on-time movement with the project.

Conclusion

Project-type grouping is a valuable but time-consuming teaching strategy and is a type of collaborative learning. Successful project group work depends on selecting tasks appropriate for long-term group work within the ability range of students yet be interesting and relevant to most students. The opportunity exists for learning not only the desired material, but also many real life skills, such as cooperating, managing, organizing, interacting, and persevering. If you try this strategy, I think you'll find that the keys to success are selecting high-functioning groups and defining the projects clearly and accurately.

Loosely Formed Groups

Loosely formed groups are often used for achieving simple tasks in the least amount of time. They are valuable for sharing information. Figure 11.7 is a guide to help you make preparations for loosely formed groups and consider some of the problems and disadvantages of the strategy.

Figure 11.7
Loosely Formed Grouping Planning at a Glance

Making Preparations	Problems and Disadvantages
• Determine a grouping strategy. • Identify an appropriate task. • Gather materials, if necessary.	• Need for greater classroom management • Less defined responsibility of group members

Making Preparations

Loosely Formed Groups
Groupings should be simple and somewhat random (e.g., a certain row, this table, that square of desks, or student choice). Most loosely formed groups work for short periods of time. Therefore, careful selection of members is not necessary.

Simple Tasks
Students are quickly grouped and tasks, such as the following, are defined:

- Discuss a topic and summarize it, list pros and cons, select most important points, or share insights.
- Have each student take a different question, find the answer, and share his or her answer with the group.
- Create a strategy for learning certain material, such as a mnemonic device, rap, song, or poem, and share the strategy with the class.

The list is really endless. Simple tasks are completed in a timely fashion because students share, discuss, and complete assignments by working together.

Appropriate Topics
Figure 11.8 gives examples of appropriate and inappropriate topics for this grouping strategy.

Figure 11.8
Loosely Formed Grouping Application Examples

Appropriate Application of Loosely Formed Grouping	Less-Effective Application of Loosely Formed Grouping
Mathematics: Study concepts for the unit test.	**Mathematics:** Complete 10 review addition problems (more efficient as partners or individuals).
Communications: Create a plot chart for a short story.	**Communications:** Research an issue from literature (better as a collaborative learning task).
Science: Create mnemonic device for information to be learned.	**Science:** Do a science experiment (would be appropriate for a quick experiment, but a lengthy experiment that was detailed would be best as project groupings).

Problems and Disadvantages

The Need for Greater Classroom Management

Because the stakes are not as high (usually this type of activity is ungraded), students may require more monitoring. However, because this type of activity may help lessen the homework burden, students may respond well and stay on task. The teacher has to monitor and make adjustments as needed.

Less-Defined Responsibility of Group Members

Group roles are not usually defined for this type of group work. Students simply work together to complete a task. On the other hand, it may help to suggest a few simple roles, such as a recorder and a leader, to promote cooperation.

Conclusion

Having students work in loosely formed groups saves time and is valuable for completing simple tasks. It can be used often without students complaining about their group because the work is usually ungraded and is in preparation for a more difficult activity. It is to the students' advantage to cooperate. If you use this type of grouping, you'll find it is an excellent way to effectively complete tasks in a short time.

Summary

My first introduction to group work was cooperative learning. I remember chanting to myself, "High, low, middle, middle, gender, race" as I formed my first cooperative

groups. At the time, the word *ethnicity* wasn't used. Believe it or not, one of the issues about cooperative learning was the *working together* issue. Teachers had to get past the *cheating* idea and understand that it *wasn't* cheating when a student got help from group members to complete a task.

As time passed, collaborative groups and project groups entered the picture. Perhaps our school's participation in National History Day and science fairs moved us in that direction. The idea that students can work together to complete a multi-task project was new. And with this strategy came a new problem—how to grade. "A" students around the country complained bitterly about group grades because, for some, it caused them to lose their position for graduation honors. I suggest that teachers consider finding a way to assign individual grades. It prevents many hard feelings and helps motivate others to continue their task in spite of the fact they must work with one irresponsible member.

If a teacher is having problems with classroom management, it is wise to avoid group work until the problems are solved. Group work requires quality classroom management. Too much time can be wasted if students are not on task and productive. Classroom instruction time is a valuable commodity, not to be wasted on fruitless activities, and group work without good management is ineffective. However, group work properly managed is a valuable instructional tool.

> Leadership opportunities abound as quickly formed groups take on short-term tasks. Teachers need to be observant and identify possible leaders and combinations of students who work well together!

Additional Reading

If you are interested in learning more about students working in small groups, consider reading the following:

Cummings, C. (2000). *Winning strategies for classroom management* (pp. 44–55). Alexandria, VA: Association for Supervision and Curriculum Development. (Provides information on small group work.)

Harmin, M. (1994). *Inspiring active learning* (pp. 95–117). Alexandria, VA: Association for Supervision and Curriculum Development. (Covers strategies for cooperative group work, project work guidelines, and task and team skill guidelines.)

Johnson, D. W., Johnson, R. T., & Holubec, E. J. (1994). *Cooperative learning in the classroom.* Alexandria, VA: Association for Supervision and Curriculum Development. (Provides in-depth information regarding cooperative learning.)

Marzano, R., Pickering, D., & Pollack, J. (2001). *Classroom instruction that works* (pp. 84–91). Alexandria, VA: Association for Supervision and Curriculum Development. (Provides information on cooperative learning.)

Wray, D. (2001). *Classroom interaction and collaborative learning, from theory to practice.* London: Routledge. (Provides information on collaborative learning.)

12 Working in Pairs

Having children learn from one another creates powerful bonds between them and sends a message very different from that sent by a classroom in which each child is on his or her own.
—Alfie Kohn (1998, p. 241)

The interaction with the greatest opportunity to learn comes when working with pairs. Students can be paired in several ways: by unequal ability, by knowledge or talents, or at random. Students working in pairs have an opportunity for input from a peer without the need for the higher-level social skills required in small groups. For those who have a trust issue with adults, pairing provides an opportunity to learn without those issues interfering with the acquisition of knowledge or skills.

Student Mentors (Unequal Pairings)

Deliberate pairings of students with unequal skills is done with the purpose of providing a ready mentor, and can be handled in several ways. The students could work together, or the mentor could be available when needed for tutoring and advising.

Figure 12.1 is a guide to help you make preparations for student mentors and consider some of the problems and disadvantages of the strategy.

Figure 12.1
Student Mentor Planning at a Glance

Making Preparations	Problems and Disadvantages
• Match workable pairs according to personality and ability. • Give statement of expectations. • Gather necessary materials.	• Mentor has increased responsibilities. • Tutored students may become too reliant on mentor. • Mentor lacks skills necessary for sharing what he or she knows.

Making Preparations

In unequal pairings, teachers are asking two students to work together for a period of time. Although they need not be friends, they should not have unresolved conflicts. In addition, the mentor's skills should be strong enough to give appropriate, accurate guidance.

The teacher should clearly define what is expected of the mentoring and mentored students:

- Both mentor and mentored should understand the basic courtesy and work ethic needed when working in pairs.
- The mentor should have a clear understanding of the information to be taught.
- The mentored student should learn good questioning skills for sharing needs. ("I don't understand this" is not a question and is not helpful in providing clues for the mentor.)

Appropriate Topics

Figure 12.2 gives examples of appropriate and inappropriate topics for the student mentors.

Problems and Disadvantages

Being a mentor may mean the student will need to put aside work to help a classmate. Some students may not deal well with the increased responsibility of helping others along with their regular work. If a student's needs become too demanding for the mentor, consider the following options:

- Rotate mentors for students who require frequent help (weekly, for instance).

A student quietly points to a printed word. Whispering occurs, information is exchanged, and soon both students are back on task. Immediate help has been offered with a minimum of disruption. That's how unequal pairing can work even in the lower grades.

- Assign more than one mentor for the needy student and have them alternate.
- Provide a way for the mentor to privately inform the teacher when the obligations become too burdensome.

The purpose of mentoring is to help the student acquire the skills to become more independent. Sometimes the mentored student becomes too reliant on the mentor, and expected growth does not occur. If this happens, possible solutions include:

- Removing the mentor and having the mentored student work with the teacher, who can help him learn when and how to ask questions.
- Changing mentors to see if different personalities will solve the problem.
- Working with the original pair to help both gain skills for working in the mentor-mentored environment.

Figure 12.2
Student Mentor Application Examples

Appropriate Application of Student Mentors	Less-Effective Application of Student Mentors
Mathematics: Work on daily math assignment for the purpose of reinforcing knowledge already mastered by most students.	**Mathematics:** Do assignments in which math skills are new to the mentor. (Mentor needs to learn skills first.)
Communications: Provide reading help by identifying and explaining words in the text.	**Communications:** Complete an assessment of comprehension. (Testing results may be invalid.)

Understanding the information does not mean that the mentor knows how to share it. Some students don't have the skills to teach or the patience to work with a student with low skills. One good idea is to match less-skilled mentors with students who have fewer needs. Students will then not feel left out, and will have fewer demands imposed on them. In addition, the mentor will have less stressful opportunities to develop mentoring skills. Another suggestion is to allow students who have negative feelings about mentoring to opt out, perhaps providing them with a partner of equal ability or allowing them to work alone.

Conclusion

Mentoring can be a valuable strategy for the classroom, but it shouldn't be over-used. Mentors have a big responsibility, and they could experience burnout if over-burdened. Pairing in mentorship is important and should happen after a teacher has achieved a good understanding of her students and their skills, personalities, strengths, and weaknesses. It is important to be flexible when using mentoring. If a quality mentor is having a bad day and needs a break, a way of providing for that need should be made available.

Student Partnerships

Students selected for partnerships have an equal responsibility to work together, either in a "study-buddy" or task-oriented format. There are a wide variety of advantages to working successfully in partnerships, including speed of completion, more diverse points of view, and greater opportunity to participate. In addition, there are many appropriate tasks for working in student pairs.

Figure 12.3 is a guide to help you make preparations for the student-pairs strategy and consider some of the problems and disadvantages.

> A touch of social opportunity, possible backup tutor if needed, opportunity for choices and sharing while decreasing the work-load—sounds like a solid strategy for learn-ing! This approach is perfect for middle and high school students.

Figure 12.3
Student Pairs Planning at a Glance

Making Preparations	Problems and Disadvantages
• Match pairs according to task. • Gather appropriate information and materials. • Provide guidance as needed.	• Need for greater classroom management • Greater responsibility in pairing

---

Making Preparations

Partnerships are not based on unequal abilities, but rather on selecting pairs to accomplish a task. Student partners may have equal ability, but maybe not in the same areas. If a task requires a variety of skills, pairs may be selected to best meet those demands. The student pairs should be able to form a working relationship; as with mentoring, it is best not to match students with best friends or social enemies.

Partnerships can tackle nearly any classroom task. It is important to provide clear assignments and adequate information of what is expected and when it is due. Lengthy assignments and projects should include a checklist with a timeline showing due dates.

Appropriate Topics

Figure 12.4 gives examples of appropriate and inappropriate topics for student pairs.

Figure 12.4
Student Pairs Application Examples

Appropriate Application of Student Pairs	Less-Effective Application of Student Pairs
Mathematics: Practice math skills.	Most activities are appropriate for partnerships.
Communications: Study for a vocabulary test.	
Science: Do a science fair project or work as lab partners.	

Problems and Disadvantages

When having students work with partners instead of small groups, teachers need to adjust to the increased demands for guidance and assistance. It is essential for teachers to circulate, monitoring for progress and misconduct. On the other hand, because there is less potential for social problems between two students than in a group, there may also be fewer conflicts.

In group work, one student may be responsible for recording, one for leadership, one for material handling, and so forth. In pairing, each partner must take on more responsibility, and the roles are generally less defined because the partners must decide how to complete the whole task. When one slacks off in a group, others share the extra burden; if one does not help carry the load in a partnership, the partner has no help.

Conclusion

"With your study buddy, complete the questions on page 10. You will be responsible for dividing the task in a fair manner or jointly doing the entire task. You have two minutes to move to your assigned area. Work will be handed in at the end of the period. If you finish early, begin learning the material." With instructions as simple as those, students can be working on an assignment. Of course, it will move a little more smoothly when students have a definite routine with a standard of behavior. Student pairs often fall into a proficient working pattern for completing assignments. When well paired, much can be accomplished in a short amount of time. But when students work together, you'll find that they may fall back into poor habits if not supervised. Teacher monitoring is important.

Random Pairing

Random pairing is a convenience. It works best when used on a short-term basis because little thought is given to pairing for the needs of the student or the demands of the task. The real advantage of random pairing is that it saves time. Figure 12.5 is a guide to help you make preparations for the student-pairing strategy and consider some of the problems and disadvantages.

Figure 12.5
Random Pairing Planning at a Glance

Making Preparations	**Problems and Disadvantages**
• Determine an appropriate task. • Decide on an appropriate pairing strategy (student choice, seat partners, counting off, and so forth). • Gather necessary materials.	• Classroom management issues as random pairing may be harder to control than assigned pairings • Not effective for difficult or involved tasks as student pairs may not have needed skills and knowledge

Making Preparations

"With your neighbor, discuss this issue and decide what factors made a difference to the conclusion," says the teacher. This type of quickly formed pairing has a definite place in the classroom. It requires no real preparation; pairs can be created according to student choice, proximity, or count-offs.

The kinds of activity to be done with random pairings are simple ones, such as

- Creating a list of the important factors of a topic.
- Solving a problem using a new formula.
- Finding the answer to a question in the textbook and paraphrasing or summarizing the information.
- Helping each other learn a poem, formula, or how to spell words (i.e., any everyday school task).
- Listing the pros and cons of an issue being studied.
- Sharing what has been learned.

The above examples support the teaching, can help with the application of learning, and may require only a few minutes of class time.

Appropriate Topics

Figure 12.6 gives examples of appropriate and inappropriate topics for randomly paired groupings.

Figure 12.6

Random Pairing Application Examples

Appropriate Application of Random Pairing	Less-Effective Application of Random Pairing
Social Studies: Paraphrase the Preamble of the Constitution.	**Social Studies:** Make project boards (skills and knowledge may be missing from random pairings).
Communications: Create a plot chart for a short story.	**Communications:** Edit and revise written composition (level of knowledge for editing and revision may be missing from pairs).
Science: Using magnets and iron filings, discover different patterns that are made by moving the magnets under the paper.	**Science:** Do science fair projects (skills and knowledge may be missing).

Problems and Disadvantages

Whenever students are required to move, as would be necessary for pairing, there will be some confusion. A good procedure is to provide time restrictions. "You have two minutes to quietly gather your materials, move to your new place of work, and begin the task." Proximity techniques are helpful in getting the students on task. When working with permanent pairings, seating arrangements and procedures can be planned and become routine. When working with random pairs, the very fact that the pairing is random may cause confusion—for example, pairing according to student choice can leave some students without partners, as can pairing according to proximity (if there is no one in the desk beside a student). Random pairings are not efficient for involved, difficult tasks. There are too many opportunities to pair students who have personality conflicts and who together don't have the skills necessary for the defined task.

Conclusion

"With your neighbor, think, pair, share," the teacher advises after discussing an issue. "The topic to be considered is recorded on the board. Move your chairs, and decide on a recorder. You'll have six minutes to complete the task." Providing quality directions is one of the best techniques for reducing classroom management problems and for obtaining quality results from the effort. Time constraints are also helpful in increasing the level of student concern.

Summary

When I first allowed students to work in pairs, one of the first questions I heard, amazingly, was, "You don't call this cheating?" Even students had to get past the belief that providing an opportunity for extra help was the same as cheating. I then had to explain that if they wanted to work in pairs they needed to each carry their share of the load and this is what made it fair. They accepted that explanation and realized that I meant what I said. If at any time I observed one person in a pair not participating, I gave fair warning; if the warning was not heeded, I provided consequences.

Teachers looking for a way to promote cooperation, hasten completion of a task, or provide peer support should consider pairing. One advantage of this strategy is that teachers can use different kinds of pairing at the same time: some students can be paired with mentors, whereas others might be paired with the purpose of supplying the skills needed to complete the task. It might even be a good idea for students to have some input before assigning partners by having them answer two questions: "Who do you know you could work with well—not friends, but good coworkers?" and "Is there anyone you are certain you could *not* work with? You may list only one." I've always honored the list of peers with whom students said they could not work. It prevented me from making poor selections for my students. With partnerships where it is one-on-one, a cordial relationship is important.

Additional Reading

If you are interested in learning more about students working in pairs, consider reading the following:

Cummings, C. (2000). *Winning strategies for classroom management* (pp. 48–50). Alexandria, VA: Association for Supervision and Curriculum Development. (Provides additional information on paired learning.)

Robbins, P. (1991). *How to plan and implement a peer coaching program.* Alexandria, VA: Association for Supervision and Curriculum Development. (Gives in-depth information on peer coaching.)

Topping, K., & Ehly, S. (Eds.). (1998). *Peer-assisted learning.* Mawah, NJ: Lawrence Erlbaum Associates. (Contains a collection of information from various contributors regarding the benefits of peer-assisted learning.)

The industrious 3rd grader says, "I'll do 1–3, and you do 4–6. We'll both work on 7. It is the hardest one." Quick planning and sharing the load make everyday tasks seem less tedious.

13

Working As an Individual

*The successful student is one who learns how to use research
materials, libraries, note cards, and computer files, as well as
knowledgeable parents, teachers, older students and classmates,
in order to master those tasks of schools that are not transparently
clear ... and makes use of the intelligence distributed throughout
his environment.*

—Howard Gardner (1991, p. 136)

With this strategy, the individual works alone to learn, practice a skill, and show proof of learning. The advantages are that the work can be individualized to fit the needs of the student without too much difficulty, and the pace in which the student learns can be adjusted with ease. In the traditional classroom, it was common to see the teacher at the front of the room providing instruction and then assigning seatwork to be completed individually by the students. That type of learning still exists along with a wide variety of other strategies for working as an individual to learn and assess.

Independent Seatwork

When students have learned skills or knowledge, independent seatwork may be used to practice it and ascertain the level of understanding. The success of this strategy depends on the quality of instruction and how much the student has learned.

Figure 13.1 is a guide to help you make preparations for independent seatwork and consider some of the problems and disadvantages of the strategy.

> **Figure 13.1**
> Independent Seatwork Planning at a Glance
>
> | Making Preparations | Problems and Disadvantages |
> |---|---|
> | • Assess whether students are ready for independent work.
• Gather necessary materials.
• Provide adequate instructions (visual/audio). | • One-on-one time with the teacher is limited
• Time for completing assignments varies among students |

Making Preparations

When preparing for independent seatwork, the materials should be made ready. Sometimes, making a note of the text page or workbook along with exercises or problems to be assigned is all that is needed. If worksheets are required, adequate copies should be prepared. If manipulatives are to be used, then those should be made available. Machine-scored answer sheets are handy and may be used for worksheets and assessments in multiple-choice, true-false, yes-no, and matching formats. An answer sheet needs to be prepared for the electronic scoring key, and students will need to have No. 2 pencils.

Students will be working independently, so they will not have each other for a resource if they cannot remember instructions. It is wise to present instructions orally and in written format, such as on the chalkboard or on a transparency. Examples of the work to be completed are sometimes beneficial, especially if the material is relatively new or detailed. A question-and-answer time before the assignment can be a good approach, but questions may be so individualized that it would be a waste of class time to answer questions with the whole group. This is often an on-the-spot teacher decision.

Appropriate Topics

Figure 13.2 gives examples of appropriate and inappropriate topics for the independent seatwork.

Problems and Disadvantages

If the independent seatwork is an assessment, one-on-one time with the teacher may not be an issue. Students are on their own to prove what they have learned. Teacher monitoring takes priority over teacher instruction. However, if the individual seatwork is for practice in mastering information, the teacher will be in demand. Waiting for help is sometimes difficult for struggling or anxious students; they should learn coping skills, such as moving on to a section they can do while

"I don't get it." "What does this mean?" "What did I do wrong?" Working with students as individuals is a challenging and demanding task. Sometimes assigning the most needy students a peer tutor will help you make yourself available to others in need of help.

waiting for teacher input. If there are high-demand students in the room, this might be a good time to implement student tutors who can quickly answer the simple questions.

"What am I supposed to do now?" students often ask when they finish minutes after the work was assigned. One of the most difficult management problems with individual seatwork is the varied time allocations students need to complete a task—some are just getting started, while others, well into the task, and others still are already done. Whatever the teacher decides to do, students should not perceive that they are being penalized for working quickly and accurately. Anything they are asked to do during individual seatwork should not be busy work. This might be an excellent time for independent learning centers, moving to the reading center, or some other teacher-designed learning activity readily available to the students.

Conclusion

Independent seatwork places responsibility for proof of learning directly on the student. It should be used after students have attained some level of comfort with the knowledge or skill.

Figure 13.2
Independent Seatwork Application Examples

Appropriate Application of Independent Seatwork	Less-Effective Application of Independent Seatwork
Mathematics: Practice math skills.	**Mathematics:** Learn a new math skill.
Communications: Write an essay.	**Communications:** Learn how to write quality introductions for essays.

Computer-Assisted Instruction

Computer-assisted instruction (CAI) is an excellent choice for skills practice in any subject. Quality programs are available, and when they are aligned to the needs of students and the curriculum, students can benefit greatly from them. Such programs are generally designed to test for mastery, and therefore allow the teacher greater freedom to teach the more abstract, difficult concepts. An additional advantage of CAI is that, because students generally enjoy computer activities, they come to the computer with a positive attitude. In addition, CAI offers immediate feedback with the possibility of immediate tutoring.

Figure 13.3 is a guide to help you make preparations for computer-assisted instruction and consider some of the problems and disadvantages of the strategy.

Making Preparations

Most schools have uniform rules for computer use (e.g., for logging in and out, passwords, and respecting equipment). Whenever using computers, it is wise to make sure students understand their responsibility to abide by the rules designated by the school and by the teacher. When new students come into the classroom, they will need to be taught the rules for computer use.

In some schools computers are placed in a lab or in the library. This means that the teacher has to plan ahead to sign up for the computers and make travel plans. If only some of the class can use the computers, the teacher needs to plan a way to ensure that students will arrive and return without causing disruption in the halls, will have some expertise with the program they use, and understand conduct expectations in the new environment. If each classroom has a few computers per room, the teacher will need to decide whether to borrow stations in additional classrooms so that all students can work at the computer or whether to provide a rotating plan for students' computer access.

The 1st grader's eyes were dancing with delight as glorious graphics and sounds celebrated his success mastering the program. The fascination with the computer is an advantage that teachers need to use!

Figure 13.3
Computer-Assisted Instruction Planning at a Glance

Making Preparations	**Problems and Disadvantages**
• Establish computer rules. • Schedule computer availability. • Check on program availability by making sure that program license covers the number of students in the class.	• Limited number of computers • "Bargain" programs that are flawed • Programs that provide only one test to assess mastery

---

When a program has been selected, the next consideration is the number of licenses for the program. When schools purchase programs, they usually purchase a maximum-use number. If this number is small, the teacher might want to make sure others on the faculty realize that the class will be using the licensed number during a certain period of time. The person in charge of computers in the building usually can provide license information.

Appropriate Topics

Figure 13.4 gives examples of appropriate and inappropriate topics for computer-assisted instruction.

Figure 13.4

Computer-Assisted Instruction Application

Appropriate Application of Computer-Assisted Instruction	Less-Effective Application of Computer Assisted Instruction
Mathematics: Practice math facts or apply formulas.	Using any program that doesn't meet the needs of the students and the curriculum.
Communications: Practice grammar and punctuation skills.	

Problems and Disadvantages

Concerns regarding the number of usable computers take into account the number in need of repair. Available computers may include the "bargain basement" ones that schools buy because they are inexpensive. Sometimes the memory on these is too limited to operate some of the high-memory programs. It is possible that such computers are mixed in with the general collection of computers in a school, so it is wise to check whether the program will work on the computers you plan to use.

It is also possible that the program will not do well what it claims it can do. If a program is new, then as with all audiovisual formats, the teacher should preview it. If possible, new programs should be purchased with the right to return them if they don't meet expectations. Programs that are networked are too expensive to settle for ones that are somehow flawed.

Programs often have tests to assess student mastery. If students don't pass the first time, then students will need to retest. It is important to determine whether programs use the same test each time or if it has a bank of questions that are rotated into tests. This prevents students memorizing the answers to the test instead of learning the material. If a program is already purchased and it uses the same test over and over, then the teacher will need to provide an alternative method to assess mastery after completing the tutorial. If the program provides a different test each time, the teacher can use the assessment from the computer program.

Conclusion

CAI is a timesaving strategy for teachers that provides valuable instruction for the students if quality programs are available. There is the added benefit that while some students are using the computer, others can be receiving personalized instruction from the teacher.

Learning Centers and Interactive Bulletin Boards

Teachers often create learning centers or interactive bulletin boards for student use. These strategies generally need specific rules and some practice by students in following those rules, but can be very effective because they can vary in difficulty to meet the individual needs of the students. Teachers can provide material for the high-, middle-, and low-skilled students in one area by offering a variety of options at each center.

Figure 13.5 is a guide to help you make preparations for learning centers and interactive bulletin boards and consider some of the problems and disadvantages of the strategy.

Figure 13.5
Learning Centers and Interactive Bulletin Boards Planning at a Glance

Making Preparations	**Problems and Disadvantages**
• Prepare center materials for independent-work on skills or knowledge. • Prepare written rules and instructions for each activity. • Determine how to keep records of student use and how to assess student work.	• Availability of center space so several students can work at the same time • Adequate time to accomplish an assignment in one session at the center • Time for making center materials and putting up bulletin boards

---

Making Preparations

If the teacher makes the learning centers instead of purchasing premade materials, then preparation time is needed. When creating the centers, options for the various levels of students should be considered. This can be done by sorting the level of work ahead of time (e.g., questions of a lower level found in one place, such as among the first five questions or the odd-numbered ones). Another option for sorting levels is preparing folders with similar activities at varied ability levels. Because learning centers and interactive bulletin boards are designed to be independent activities, to ignore the ability levels of students would be self-defeating.

Once the centers or interactive bulletin boards have been designed, any unique directions should be considered and, when necessary, notations made to model them when they are presented. If the teacher normally has centers or boards in the classroom, then generic rules of use should be in place already.

Some learning centers and interactive bulletin boards are designed to provide immediate feedback; in these cases, grading center work is not really necessary.

Keeping records of who has had the opportunity to use the center would, however, be important. This could be done by simply providing a checklist of names near the center that the students check each time they have had an opportunity to use the center or its various components.

Appropriate Topics

Figure 13.6 gives examples of appropriate and inappropriate topics for learning centers and interactive bulletin boards.

Figure 13.6
Learning Centers and Interactive Bulletin Boards Application Examples

Appropriate Application of Learning Centers and Interactive Bulletin Boards	Less-Effective Application of Learning Centers and Interactive Bulletin Boards
Communications: Work with interactive bulletin board materials that provide immediate feedback to learning the parts of speech.	Any learning center or interactive bulletin board is effective if it meets the needs of the students and curriculum.
Science: Create task centers with quick learning tasks to help support learning objectives such as learning the parts of an atom.	

Problems and Disadvantages

Do students go to the center when they are done with their seatwork and need something to do while waiting for others? If so, when will the slower-moving students get this opportunity? Perhaps one solution is to rotate activities. This will guarantee that *all* students have the opportunity to visit the learning centers and interactive bulletin boards.

Making quality learning centers or interactive bulletin boards is time-consuming. Because students are expected to work independently, careful consideration of what students are capable of doing must be made during the preparation stage. In addition to deciding how to present the material, teachers must ensure that the material is adequate for the range of students' abilities existing within the classroom. It would be a good decision to make reusable materials whenever possible (e.g., laminate sheets and use dry erase markers or transparency pens). Centers could also be assembled using presentation boards so teachers could store them to use for another year without much extra work. The closed presentation boards could be labeled clearly to be easily identified in a storage area.

Conclusion

Learning centers and interactive bulletin boards enrich the learning atmosphere of the classroom. They offer the opportunity to meet the varied abilities of students and allow for self-pacing.

Working with Manipulatives

Immediate-feedback manipulatives are effective teaching tools. They have the advantage, as does CAI, that students *do not have the opportunity to learn and practice the wrong answer.* Some manipulatives are designed to help as tools for finding the answer but do not provide immediate feedback. These manipulatives are helpful, but the teacher must monitor closely to see that students understand how to use them and are obtaining correct answers and results.

Figure 13.7 is a guide to help you make preparations for using manipulatives and consider some of the problems and disadvantages of the strategy.

"When do I get to go to the new center?" the anxious 2nd grader inquires. The area looks inviting and fun, but learning lurks behind the well-planned activities. Capitalize on that enthusiasm and make learning centers strong on *learning* behind that "glitter."

Figure 13.7
Manipulatives Planning at a Glance

Making Preparations	**Problems and Disadvantages**
• Make or obtain manipulatives. • Provide instructions for managing and using the manipulatives.	• Time consuming to make and manage • Increased demand for teacher monitoring

---

Making Preparations

Manipulatives may be purchased or designed by the teacher to meet a particular need. If the teacher prepares the manipulatives, she should plan the time to do so. Expenses must be considered for purchasing commercial manipulatives or materials to assemble teacher-made ones. If they are available somewhere in the district, then teachers should follow procedures for reserving them.

If the manipulatives are small, putting sets into plastic bags that seal with a zip or slide might be a good managing tool. Numbering the plastic bags is helpful for checking out sets, keeping track of who has the materials, and making sure all materials are returned. Teachers should think about possible problems of using manipulatives and decide on a solution for as many as possible (e.g., little blocks may not be tossed around the room). Because manipulatives are varied in kind and purpose, it is important to establish generic rules for use and then add specific rules as needed. Exact instructions, demonstrations, and teacher modeling may be advantageous in preparing the class for successful use.

Appropriate Topics

Figure 13.8 gives examples of appropriate and inappropriate topics for manipulatives.

Figure 13.8
Manipulatives Planning at a Glance

Appropriate Application of Manipulatives	Less-Effective Application of Manipulatives
Mathematics: Use connecting cubes or place-value blocks to solve problems.	Any manipulative that fits the needs of the student and matches the curriculum is appropriate.
Science: Have students work with word-puzzle cards to learn vocabulary terms.	

Problems and Disadvantages

If manipulatives must be made, the teacher might consider ways to lengthen the lives of these resources. Laminating paper products and spray-painting wood and wood products will protect them, so a few extra minutes of preparation may save time in the future. Obtaining help from other willing hands, such as another teacher, will also help cut down on time needed to prepare.

As with most things added to a classroom, the manipulatives must have the following:

- A storage area (temporary or permanent)
- A distribution method (e.g., first person in a row picks up and distributes materials for the row)
- A check-out and check-in method for students to take manipulatives home (if needed)
- A method for checking that complete sets are returned with no missing parts

When students have manipulatives on their desks, there will be a demand for more teacher monitoring. Such monitoring will allow the teacher to discover any problems with understanding how to correctly use the manipulatives and will help prevent classroom management problems.

Conclusion

Manipulatives are concrete teaching aids that are helpful as teaching tools. They constitute a very important strategy for the tactile-kinesthetic and visual learners who need to do and see to learn. In addition, manipulatives that provide immediate feedback, such as word puzzles, prevent students from learning incorrect answers.

Summary

There are many ways students can work independently; the trick is in knowing what works with a particular class. I've had some at-risk students who only became confident enough to work alone when they felt they had mastered the material and were ready to practice for assessment. Discovery and learning activities were done as small groups and partnerships.

Section Summary

You've arranged your room and posted your schedule. You've determined the rules your students must follow to make the classroom learning friendly. You have a plan for dealing with difficult situations. You're ready to teach. It should be simple now, but in reality it is as complicated as the students we teach. For each lesson, you must not only decide what will be taught, but how it will be presented. Success comes in selecting the strategy that fits the students and the information to be learned. As a teacher you must know your students well enough to select strategies to help them build the knowledge, skills, and confidence to become independent workers. Yes, the best strategy *is the one that works for your students. Make informed choices.*

Additional Reading

If you are interested in learning more about students working individually, consider reading the following:

Cummings, C. (2000). *Winning strategies for classroom management* (pp. 36–37). Alexandria, VA: Association for Supervision and Curriculum Development. (Direct instruction is discussed in this resource.)

Marzano, R., Pickering, D., & Pollack, J. (2001). *Classroom instruction that works* (pp. 29–48, 118–120). Alexandria, VA: Association for Supervision and Curriculum Development. (Discusses summarizing, note-taking, and advanced organizers.)

Imagine if you will a student offering to help distribute needed supplies to the class. What age would you attribute to that student? The truth is students of all ages are willing to help with the management of manipulatives. Capitalize on volunteer labor and save time!

Conclusion

In the preface to this book, we suggested that it is time to take a new look at classroom management in light of new research findings about teaching and learning, new ideas about how to help students develop responsibility for themselves, and new information on matching instructional strategies to student needs and curriculum objectives. We proposed a proactive approach aimed at preventing problems and avoiding those issues that continue to trouble both new and veteran teachers.

We chose to view the three key elements of classroom management—efficient use of time and classroom space; implementation of strategies that influence students to make good choices, rather than ones that attempt to control student behavior; and wise choice and effective implementation of instructional strategies—in separate sections of the book in order to share specific ideas relevant to each element and identify the relationships among them. We believe that this approach can help you to better analyze problems and determine whether they stem from environmental, relationship, or instructional issues.

We believe that good management strategies

- Increase student achievement.
- Make your work easier and your classroom a rich and inviting environment.
- Help you better match instructional strategies to content and student needs.
- Allow you more time to focus on *teaching* students rather than simply *managing* them.

We sincerely hope that the ideas and strategies suggested in the book help you make your classroom a rich and stimulating environment for you and your students—one in which you feel a sense of accomplishment every day as you help your students achieve to their fullest potential.

—*The Authors*

Bibliography

Adams, R. S., & Biddle, B. J. (1970). *Realities of teaching: Exploration with videotape.* New York: Holt, Rinehart, & Winston.

American Federation of Teachers. (n.d.). *Classroom procedures checklist.* Washington, DC: Educational Research and Dissemination Program.

Avalon West School District. (2003). *Student lockers and other assigned property.* Retrieved March 23, 2003, from http://www.awsb.ca/index.htm.

Boykin, M. R. (1997, August). Reading, 'riting, 'rithmitic, and respect. *Los Angeles Times.*

Bronfenbrenner, U. (1970). *Two worlds of childhood.* New York: Russell Sage Foundation.

Brophy, J. (1999). Perspectives of classroom management: Yesterday, today, and tomorrow. In H. Jerome Freiberg (Ed.), *Beyond behaviorism: Changing the class management paradigm* (pp. 43–56). Needham Heights, MA: Allyn and Bacon.

Brophy, J. (1995). *Teaching problem students.* New York: Guilford Press.

Brophy, J. (1988). Educating teachers about managing classrooms and students. *Teaching and Teacher Education, 4*(1), 1–18.

Buchanan, L. (1996). Planning the multimedia classroom. *MultiMedia Schools, 3*(4), 16–21.

Burmark, L. (2002). *Visual literacy: Learn to see, see to learn.* Alexandria, VA: Association for Supervision and Curriculum Development.

Canady, R. L., & Rettig, M. D. (1995). *Block scheduling: A catalyst for change in high schools.* Princeton, NJ: Eye on Education.

Cangelosi, J. S. (1993). *Classroom management strategies: Gaining and maintaining students' cooperation* (2nd ed.). White Plains, NY: Longman Publishing Group.

Carbo, M., Dunn, R., & Dunn, K. (1986). *Teaching students to read through their individual learning styles.* Englewood Cliffs, NJ: Prentice-Hall.

Carroll, J. M. (1994). Organizing time to support learning. *The School Administrator, 51*(3), 26–28, 30–33.

Cawelti, G. (1994). *High school restructuring: A national study.* Arlington, VA: Educational Research Service: ED 366 070.

Costa, A. L., & Garmston, R. J. (1994). *Cognitive coaching: A foundation for renaissance schools.* Norwood, MA: Christopher-Gordon Publishers.

Cullum, A. (1971). *The geranium on the windowsill just died but teacher you just went right on.* Virginia, MN: Harlin Quist.

Cummings, C. (2000). *Winning strategies for classroom management.* Alexandria, VA: Association for Supervision and Curriculum Development.

Cummings, C. (1996). *Managing to teach: A guide to classroom management* (2nd ed.). Edmonds, WA: Teaching, Inc.

Drucker, P. F. (1954). *The practice of management.* New York: Harper.

Edwards, C., Gandini, L., & Forman, G. (1993). *The hundred languages of children.* Westport, CT: Ablex.

Edwards, C. H. (1993). *Classroom discipline and management.* New York: Macmillan Publishing.

ERIC Clearinghouse on Disabilities and Gifted Education. (1989). *Meeting the needs of able learners through flexible pacing.* Educational Research Service: ED 314916. Arlington, VA. Retrieved October 23, 2002, from http://ericec.org/digests/e464.html.

Evertson, C., Emmer, E., & Worsham, M. (2000). *Classroom management for elementary teachers* (5th ed.). Needham Heights, MA: Allyn and Bacon.

Evertson, C. M., Emmer, E. T., Clements, B. S., & Worsham, M. E. (1994). *Classroom management for elementary teachers.* Needham Heights, MA: Allyn and Bacon.

Fay, J., & Funk, D. (1995). *Teaching with love and logic.* Golden, CO: Love and Logic Press.

First class gradebook. (2003). Retrieved November 11, 2002, from http://www.win-planet.com/winplanet/reviews/654/1/screenshot314.

Froyen, L. A. (1993). *Classroom management: The reflective teacher-leader.* New York:Macmillan.

Gardner, H. (1991). *The unschooled mind: How children think and how schools should teach.* New York: BasicBooks.

Gootman, M. E. (1997). *The caring teacher's guide to discipline.* Thousand Oaks, CA: Corwin Press.

Hunter, M. (1990). *Discipline that develops self-discipline.* El Segundo, CA: TIP Publications.

Johnson, D., & Johnson, R. (1984). *Circles of learning: Cooperation in the classroom.* Alexandria, VA: Association for Supervision and Curriculum Development.

Johnstone, A. H., & Percival, F. (1976). Attention breaks in lectures. *Education in Chemistry, 13,* 49–50.

Jones, F. H. (1987). *Positive classroom discipline.* New York: McGraw-Hill.

Jones, V. F., & Jones, L. S. (2000). *Comprehensive classroom management.* Needham Heights, MA: Allyn and Bacon.

Jones, V. F. (1995). *Comprehensive classroom management: Creating positive learning environments for all students.* Needham, MA: Allyn and Bacon.

Kohn, A. (1998). *What to look for in a classroom.* San Francisco: Jossey-Bass.

Kohn, A. (1996). *Beyond discipline: From compliance to community.* Alexandria, VA: Association for Supervision and Curriculum Development.

Kovalik, S. (1994). *The model: Integrated thematic instruction.* Kent, WA: Susan Kovalik & Associates.

Krasner, S. (2002). *Block scheduling, school schedules, and use of time in school: Bibliography.* Retrieved November 11, 2002, from http://www.ctserc.org/library/actualbibs/BlockScheduling.pdf.

Learning Disabilities Association of America. (n.d.) *Learning disabilities resources.* Retrieved October 24, 2002, from http://www.ldanatl.org/Resource.html.

Lemlech, J. K. (1991). *Classroom management: Methods and techniques for elementary and secondary teachers.* Prospect, IL: Waveland Press.

Levin, J., & Shanken-Kaye, J. (1996). *The self-control classroom.* Dubuque, IA: Kendall/Hunt.

Maeroff, G. I. (1994). The assault on the Carnegie unit. *NCA Quarterly, 68*(3), 408–411.

Marzano, R. J. (2000). *Transforming classroom grading.* Alexandria, VA: Association for Supervision and Curriculum Development.

Marzano, R. J., Pickering, D. J., & Pollock, J. E. (2001). *Classroom instruction that works: Research-based strategies for increasing student achievement.* Alexandria, VA: Association for Supervision and Curriculum Development.

McCaslin, M., & Good, T. (1992). Compliant cognition: The misalliance of management and instructional goals in current school reform. *Educational Researcher, 21,* 4–17.

McMinn County Schools' Technology Plan. (2000). Retrieved March 23, 2003, fromhttp://www.mcminn.k12.tn.us/technology/technology.html.

National Center for Education Statistics. (1997). *Protecting the privacy of student records: Guidelines for education agencies.* Retrieved November 13, 2002, from http://www.nces.ed.gov/pubs97/p97527/index.html.

National Resource Center for Safe Schools. (2003). Retrieved October 22, 2002, from http://www.safetyzone.org.

Northwest Regional Educational Laboratory, Rural Education Program. (1990). *Literature search on the question: What are the advantages and disadvantages of various scheduling options for small secondary schools (high schools and middle schools)?* Portland, OR: Author. ED 329 385.

Rasmussen, K. (1998). Looping: Discovering the benefits of multiyear teaching. *Education Update, 40*(2). Alexandria, VA: Association for Supervision and Curriculum Development.

Red Mountain Ranch Elementary School. (n.d.) *Vertical Teams.* Retrieved November 11, 2002, from http://www.mpsaz.org/redmtnranch/Vertical_Team_Philosophy.html.

Rose, D. H., & Meyer, A. (2002). *Teaching every student in the digital age: Universal design for learning.* Alexandria, VA: Association for Supervision and Curriculum Development.

Savage, T. V. (1999). *Teaching self-control through management and discipline.* Needham Heights, MA: Allyn and Bacon.

Schonfeld, D. J., Lichenstein, R., Pruett, M. K., & Speese-Linehan, D. (2002). *How to prepare for and respond to a crisis* (2nd ed.). Alexandria, VA: Association for Supervision and Curriculum Development.

South Portland High School. (n.d.). *Student locker policy and procedure.* Retrieved November 8, 2002, from http://www.spsd.org/REDRIOT/policy/locker.htm.

Sprenger, M. (1999). *Learning and memory: The brain in action.* Alexandria, VA: Association for Supervision and Curriculum Development.

State of Wisconsin. (1998). Compulsory School Attendance and Truancy Laws, Memorandum 98–27.

Temple University Collaborative for Excellence in Teacher Preparation (CETP). (n.d.). *Classroom management: Classroom routines.* Retrieved May 18, 2002, from http://www.temple.edu/CETP/temple_teach/cm-routi.html.

United States Education Reference File. (1999). *Background note on definition of 'Carnegie unit.'* Retrieved May 13, 2002, from http://www.uta.fi/FAST/US5/REF/carnegie.html.

Villarreal-Carman, T., & Warren, B. (2001, October). *Improving student achievement through classroom observations and feedback* [seminar]. At New Teacher Center,University of California, Santa Cruz.

Wang, M. C., Haertel, G. D., & Walberg, H. J. (1993–1994). Synthesis of research: What helps students learn? *Educational Leadership, 51*(4).

Weinstein, C.S. (1979). The physical environment of the school: A review of the research. *Review of Educational Research, 49*(4), 557–610.

Welsh, S. W. (1987, March). *Classroom management* [seminar]. At Instructional Training Company, Scottsdale, Arizona.

Wiseman, J. (1995, January). *Elements of effective instruction* [seminar]. At Newport Mesa Unified School District, Newport Beach, California.

Wolfe, P. (2001). *Brain matters: Translating research into classroom practice.* Alexandria, VA: Association for Supervision and Curriculum Development.

Wong, H. K. & Wong, R. T. (1998). *The first days of school.* Mountain View, CA: Harry K. Wong Publications.

WorkSpace Resources. (1998). *Computer classroom design: The issues facing designers of computer classrooms.* Retrieved February 25, 2003, from http://www.workspace resources.com/education/cicdesi1.htm.

Index

About the Authors

Joyce McLeod speaks nationally and internationally as a consultant on issues in mathematics and science education as well as in writing and delivering professional development in mathematics. She is an author of *Harcourt Science* (2002), *Math Advantage* (1999), and *Harcourt Math* (2002), published by Harcourt School Publishers. Prior to her retirement from Harcourt School Publishers, she worked as senior vice president and editor-in-chief of the mathematics, science, and health division at Harcourt and as senior consultant in mathematics, science, and health. Since 1984, she has held a Visiting Professorship in the School of Education and Human Development at Rollins College in Winter Park, Florida. She teaches courses in the Masters of Arts in Teaching program. She has taught courses in classroom management, cognitive development, and mathematics content for elementary and middle-school teachers. McLeod is the 1991 and 2001 recipient of the Natalie Delcamp Award for Excellence in Teaching at Rollins. She also received the 1995 University of Central Florida Alumni Association Professional Achievement Award, presented by the College of Education.

Jan Fisher is a professional development consultant living in Laguna Beach, California. As a district staff developer for the Newport-Mesa Unified School District, Jan worked with new and veteran teachers in the areas of classroom management, instruction, and models of teaching, and with all staff in planning and implementing school improvement initiatives. Currently, she provides training and support in both management and instruction to the teachers and administrators in several southern California districts. She also works for the University of California, Irvine, where she teaches preservice teachers about the intricacies of class management, and assists in coordinating the California Beginning Teacher Support and Assessment Program (BTSA).

Jan received her bachelor's degree from Whitman College in Walla Walla, Washington, and her Master's degree from Pepperdine University in Malibu, California. She was honored in 1996 as an "Outstanding Contributor to Education" by the Orange County (California) Department of Education.

Jan has two daughters who are both teachers and a 1st-grade granddaughter who shows every sign that she, too, will someday join the "family business."

Joyce holds a Bachelor of Arts from the University of Central Florida, a Masters of Education in Administration and Supervision, and a Specialist in Education from Rollins College. She is the recipient of the Outstanding Graduate in Teacher Education awarded by Rollins College.

Joyce is married and has two sons and two grandchildren. She resides in Longwood, Florida.

Ginny Hoover retired after 31 years of teaching the middle grades in Kansas. She found a second career providing professional development in Six Traits, a writing model that also serves as the model for the Kansas writing assessment. She also does professional development in the areas of social studies, classroom management, and instructional strategies. Hoover is designated by the State of Kansas as a trainer of teachers for Six Traits and as the official lead trainer of teachers for Civics and Government. Recently she was asked to serve again on the Kansas Social Studies Standards Committee to revisit the state social studies standards. She maintains a Web site titled *Ginny's Educational WebPages* at http://www.geocities.com/ginnks/ to share her work and to collaborate with teachers around the world. Ginny also writes a regular column, "The Eclectic Teacher," for *Teachers Net* at http://teachers.net, and has published language arts units and teacher resources through *Teacher Time Savers* at http://teachertimesavers.com/GinnyHoover.htm. She also wrote a reference tool on Six Traits published by EDUPRESS.

Ginny received her bachelor's degree in Education from Emporia State University at Emporia, Kansas, and a master's degree in Teaching from Friends University in Wichita, Kansas. She is married with three children and one granddaughter and resides in Hutchinson, Kansas.

Related ASCD Resources

At the time of publication, the following ASCD resources were available; for the most up-to-date information about ASCD resources, go to www.ascd.org. ASCD stock numbers are noted in parentheses.

Audiotapes

Classroom Management at the Middle Grade Level by Alfred A. Arth, Judith Brough , Larry Holt, Kathleen B. Wheeler (#202239)

Conscious Classroom Management: Bringing Out the Best in Students and Teachers by Rick Smith (#202248)

Effective Discipline: Getting Beyond Rewards and Punishment (3 Live Seminars on Tape) by Marvin Marshall (#297190)

Books

Classroom Management That Works: Research-Based Strategies for Every Teacher by Robert J. Marzano with Jana S. Marzano and Debra Pickering **(NEW!)**

Guiding School Improvement with Action Research by Richard Sagor (#100047)

Winning Strategies for Classroom Management by Carol Cummings (#100052)

Multimedia

Classroom Management/Positive School Climate Topic Pack (#198219)

Classroom Management Professional Inquiry Kit (eight activity folders and a videotape) by Robert Hanson (#998059)

Dimensions of Learning Complete Program (teacher's and trainer's manuals, book, 6 videos, and an additional free video) by Robert J. Marzano and Debra J. Pickering (#614239)

Videos

Managing Today's Classroom (3 videos with facilitator's guide) by Rheta DeVries (#498027)

What Works in Schools Video Series (3 videos) by Robert J. Marzano (#403047)

For more information, visit us on the World Wide Web (http://www.ascd.org), send an e-mail message to member@ascd.org, call the ASCD Service Center (1-800-933-ASCD or 703-578-9600, then press 2), send a fax to 703-575-5400, or write to Information Services, ASCD, 1703 N. Beauregard St., Alexandria, VA 22311-1714 USA.